Making Change Easy

A Practical Guide to Changing Your Life,
Releasing Your Child Within, and
Enjoying the Wonder that is in the Present Moment

Jim Matheson

www.TheJoyofChange.com

This book is dedicated

to people who wish to be happy;

and in particular,

to those who suffer because of this wish.

Making Change Easy

Do you ever wonder why you aren't happy all the time?

Then this book is for you.

CONTENTS

Making Change Easy

Forward

Whatever was is no more.

Things have changed.

Life is change. Cultures, climates, your work, your body, your beliefs, your relationships, your finances, everything changes. Whatever is going on right now will not last. It does not matter how good or bad things are, they are going to change. That is certain, absolutely and irrevocably, for this is the very nature of life itself – change.

The key to a joyful life is not to manage the inevitable changes that come your way. The key to living a joyful life is to consciously create all events in your life. All of them.

This is possible.

So how do you do that?

That's what this book is about, creating change. Consciously. That's also what your life is all about; consciously choosing the life experience you are having each and every moment.

But things just happen, you say. I am not in control of what happens in my life. Not so. The quicker you change this core belief, the sooner your life will change for the better. You will be happier, healthier, wealthier, more joyful and successful. Not just some, but all of the time.

So here we are. At the beginning of a journey that will help you to understand why you're here, how to change your direction if you wish, and most importantly, how to consciously create your every moment for the rest of your life.

We are not just talking about how to find joy. You are about to experience exactly how everything, including joy, is created, and how you can become its creator.

Sound like a tall order?

Let's begin.

Are You Ready?

Making Change Easy

1.

Making Change Easy

Are You Ready For the Answer?

Are You Ready to Create Joy?
Discover Your Life Purpose?
Create the Life of Your Dreams?

Yes?

No?

Maybe?

If you answered no, or maybe, or perhaps later, or you are not quite sure just now, then turn on the TV, go bowling, tweet something, check out Facebook and YouTube, eat, grab a drink, read a book, watch a movie or do whatever else distracts you. If any of this changes, please read the next paragraph.

If your answer is yes, and if you really are ready, then you just might be about to experience the time of your life. You might be about to experience what happens when you go from not knowing to knowing, from ignorance to bliss. And then beyond all that. Whenever you choose.

"Huh? What do you mean, whenever I choose?"

From your question I gather that you are now ready to begin. Here we go.

Your purpose is to: *drum roll please:*

Consciously create your life. Instead of everything being a series of events that seem to just happen randomly, create your life so that these experiences occur because of you.

There, I've said it. Now you know. You don't have to keep searching any more. That didn't take very long now, did it?

"Yeah but what does that mean and how do I do it?"

The how is the easy part. Forgive everyone. Live in gratitude and love unconditionally.

As for the rest, if you want to love living a fulfilling life, accept that:

1. You created the life you are living
2. You are doing what you are supposed to be doing right now
3. You have all you are supposed to have right now
4. You know all you are supposed to know right now

And all this changes whenever you choose.
As does your purpose.

"Yeah but .... this is not the life I should be living. I should be richer, much healthier, in a better job, having a great relationship, joyful and stuff like that."

That can be what you now create:

Trumpets blare:

- by having and being aware of all your goals
- accepting responsibility for everything that happens
- being fully present here and now
- paying attention to all the messages and choices created by you, for you, in each and every moment
- making choices to act on those messages and choices now
- making choices consistent with your goals and values

"But I don't know what to do."

That is not true. What you are not sure about, you can ask or consult and find out. And pay attention to every result and outcome as these may be your best teachers.

"Ask who? Consult what?

Think for a moment.

- Books
- yourself
- your friends
- courses
- gurus
- teachers
- 'random' strangers
- the Universe
- God
- me

In the end, they all lead you to your purpose, which is always exactly what you are doing right now.

Until you change your purpose, of course.

"Could you be more specific about where I start?"

Do you believe the following statements?

1. There are no accidents
2. Every life has purpose
3. You have never made a wrong decision.

"No. How could that possibly be true?"

If you did believe it, how would your life be different?

"Well. Ok. Maybe I see what you mean. Are you saying that if I believe you about this, then I can be happier … I can be richer … I can be healthier … all that other stuff."

I am saying that the reality you live is the one you create.

And the more you accept responsibility for your creation, the more fulfilling and rewarding your life becomes.

"Does that mean I will also be happier all the time?"

If you choose. Many do not.

"AAGH! Give me a break."

Is that what you want? Every experience you ever had led you right here. Is this a good place to be?

"No. I mean this is not the life I want to be living. Well parts of it are ok but some of it sucks. A lot. This is not where I want to be."

Good. Choose that now.

"Choose what?"

Where you want to go.

"Ok .... well, I'm not quite sure where that is exactly."

Are you ready to begin?

"Yes."

You know where you have been. Right? And you know what you like, or at least what you don't like. Right?

"Yes."

Now, imagine what your life would be like if you always had more than enough money and time, and were so healthy that you literally shine like a beacon in the sky. No one ever tells you what to do and whatever you do, you feel not just happy, but joyful.

"But I don't see how that will help me get where I want to be."

Life is a process, not a result. Go with the flow for now.

You go through the process and you get the result. Hopefully you don't go through it just to get the result, although that happens anyway. This is a process. You do it and things change.

Let's look at it this way. You read lots of books on how to change, right?

"Right."

And you took some courses, right?

"Right."

And you probably did some other things too, right?

"Right."

And you did make some changes, right?

"Yeah but they didn't last. And some of them didn't turn out the way I wanted."

You make two very good points.

1. Things don't last, and

2. They don't always turn out the way you planned.

Do I have that right?

"Yes."

You are right that things don't last or stay the same. Not your body, not your house, not your choices, not your money, not your health … not anything. That is the nature of reality. Things change. Always have. Always will. The good part is that you get to choose how they change. We'll get to that part later.

Your other point is that things don't always turn out the way you planned. Is that right?

"Yeah. I want something and I get it and then it's not all I thought it would be. Or I don't get something I thought I wanted and in the end it doesn't really matter that much. Or it matters so much I feel I'll be miserable forever. Many times I think that if I do this or that, then I know what will happen but it doesn't always work out that way."

Actually it did work out the way you planned. It's just that you were not aware of all that you were planning.

"What? Are you telling me I planned for Mary to dump me? Or that I planned to get sick just before I went on vacation. Or I planned to get fired from the best job I ever had? That's not true. You have really lost me now."

Stick with me and I will explain.

Long ago, you made decisions about what your life was going to be like. You did not make these decisions consciously. In fact, many people would say it was not actually you who made these decisions.

"Who then?"

- Parents and family
- Television and radio
- People talking around you
- Teachers
- Friends and peers
- Books and films
- Your genes

Even while you were in the womb, you heard things and even though you didn't understand them, you were being programmed to react to the world in certain ways. And when you were a young child, you were told how to behave and you obeyed. And then, when you rebelled, maybe around age two, you were punished for disobeying. And from that experience, you may have decided that it's easier to get through life by doing what others tell you to do. Imagine the implications of that decision.

"I am an adult now and I can do what I want."

Exactly. You can now do whatever you choose.

"Well, not exactly whatever I choose."

Exactly what you choose, as long as you are prepared to accept the consequences of what you choose.

For example, if you choose to take something that does not belong to you, there is a natural consequence that you might be caught and imprisoned. Or that you get away with it and you could choose to be happy about that. Or you could choose to feel guilty about it if you were programmed to do so long ago.

If we are not prepared to accept the consequences, then we may make a different choice.

"I can see that. But how about getting fired; I never made that choice."

Yes you did.

"No way!"

Way. You loved that job didn't you?

"Yeah. It was my dream job. I was never happier. I loved that job."

But you lied on your expense report didn't you?

"Get a life. They could afford it. It's not like they were going to miss a few dollars. And it's not like I was stealing something. I mean everyone does it."

Did you ever imagine you could get fired for this?

"No. Of course not ... well I mean, maybe. Ok. So maybe it was stealing but I was doing a great job. I worked overtime without pay every night and most weekends. I had no personal life. Everything I did was for the company. Surely I deserved something a little extra. I mean they should not have fired me for that. I was really sorry. I offered to make amends and everything."

Actually you were really sorry you got caught. And maybe sorry you got fired. You knew before you lied that doing so could lead to your getting fired and you did it anyway. You made a decision and took a risk, the natural consequence of which was that you got fired. No real surprise there. The question you might want to ask yourself is why you lied, if on some level you knew that doing so could get you fired from your 'dream job'.

"So you are saying it was my fault I got fired?"

Yes.

"Okay. Okay. I mean I was working day and night for those guys and I guess it was too much. I get it. I don't like it but I understand how I wanted to get out of there but couldn't quit. I needed the money. I loved the prestige."

And now you have neither. I guess you didn't need them after all. Either that or you didn't believe you deserved them.

"Didn't believe I deserved them? That's not true."

Isn't it?

"No, of course not."

You created a situation that proved you did not deserve the great salary and the adulation that went with such a high profile job. It wasn't even that you got greedy – you just followed your programming. Your unconscious programming told you that you did not deserve the job and told you to do what it would take to get fired. The result was inevitable.

"Are you saying I deliberately got fired?"

Yes. Ask yourself how it is that anyone could discover your lie. You had to practically throw it in their face. The very first day on the job they spent hours talking to you about how important integrity was to their business. And you knew the only way to get out of there was to demonstrate a lack of integrity.

When you were two years old, you lied and took what you wanted. And you were punished. Now you lied and took what you wanted and you got punished. The program you are running is the same.

"Well if that is true, and I am not sure it is, then it must be time for some radically new programming."

Yes.

"Okay. But what about how I lost Mary? Don't tell me I deliberately got her to dump me. I waited all my life for her. I was in love beyond reason or measure. I would have done anything for her. We were going to get married, have kids and spend our lives together happily ever after. There is no way I was ever going to sabotage that. She left me. I was so good to her. She could not have asked for someone better than me."

Actually, she could and she did.

Was she the one for you? Perhaps. Were you the one for her? Obviously not. That happens sometimes. Did you sabotage your relationship with her?

"Are you kidding me? Absolutely not."

You mean absolutely yes.

"No. I mean absolutely not."

Let me explain.

In the beginning you were infatuated. You graduated from there to what you called love. You did everything she asked. Except for one thing. She asked you to be yourself. You did not do that.

"But I wanted to please her. I did everything for her."

That is not what she was asking you to do.

"I don't understand."

You will. You failed to recognize that her attraction to you was based on who you are, not on what you did for her. The more you did things for her, the less you expressed who you are. You became like her servant. She did not need that. Nor did she want it. In the end you lost her because you lost yourself.

"Oh my God."

What else?

"How about that vacation? I was all ready to go on this great cruise and I got the worst cold ever. It turned into pneumonia and I couldn't go. Was that my choice?"

Did you pay for the trip with a credit card?

"Yes. What has that got to do with it?"

Did you have the money to pay for the trip when you booked it?

"No. but I was going to pay for it over time."

Could you afford the trip?

"Well ... I mean I really needed to go. I needed that trip. I had worked hard. I was tired. I ..."

You knew you could not afford it and you chose a way to get out of going.

"If you are so smart, how come you are here talking with me."

I have been where you are. I have walked in your shoes. I know where you can go if you choose. I would like to help you get there.

"Where can I go if I choose?"

Where indeed.

"You mean the choices are limitless?"

Yes.

Let's get started.

Making Change Easy

Are You Really Ready?
Answering These Questions Might Change Your Life.

1. How do I know if I am doing the right thing?

2. What would happen if I really understood all there is to know?

3. How can I make a difference in the world?

4. How do I go from feeling insignificant to all powerful, or at least happy?

5. Is there really such a thing as a state of bliss and if there is, how do I get there?

6. How can I end war? Or famine or torture?

7. What part of me kept me from being more successful? Is that part continuing to serve my goals?

8. If I knew there would be no tomorrow, that the world would end soon, how would I spend my day today? Or the next week, the next year?

9. If I knew that I would live forever, what would I do differently today?

10. How do I get over all the bad stuff that has happened to me?

11. How is it possible for me to be happy no matter what happens?

12. How do I know whether anything I believe is true?

13. How do I find out what my life purpose is?

14. How do I get over being so angry and hurt inside?

15. How do I get past feeling sad?

16. How can I accept what is?

17. How can I accept what is, if I know I'm going to change it?

18. Is there some magic formula or course I can take to make me feel better?

19. How can I become more competent, confident and successful?

20. Does anything really matter? If so, what?

23. Who is in charge of the world?

Remember:

You are ready. You know that because you are here.

You will discover your purpose

You are creating the life of your dreams

You Are Not Broken

2.

Making Change Easy

You Are Not Broken
You Do Not Need Fixing

Every Decision You Ever Made Was the Right One.
Your Results to Date Reflect Your True Beliefs.
You are a Master Creator.

Do you believe that?

"No, of course not. It's ridiculous."

Is it?

You created every circumstance and event in your life. Without exception. And if that is true, and it is, then you can create your life anew in any moment you choose.

"I think you lost me at hello. I mean get real. What the heck are you talking about? I created nothing. Oh sure I can see what you were getting at when you talked about how I got fired or lost my girlfriend, but really, it's more than a bit of a stretch to say that I created everything in my life so far."

If you didn't create it, who did?

"Life did. I mean life is obviously a random set of experiences that just happen. You know. Shit happens. Luck happens. Life happens. It's short. It's sweet or crappy and then you die. That's it. End of story."

It that were true, and it's not, then what would be the purpose of life?

"The purpose of life my friend is to survive, to go on, till we die."

And then what?

"What are you going on about? Life ends when you do. That's it. Finis. It's over. It ends when it ends. There is no more. And even if there were, and there really is reincarnation, you just do it again. There is no point. There is no purpose. There is no grand direction other than to exist."

Finally we agree.

"We do?"

Yes. The purpose of life is to exist.

"Yeah but why? What's the point of existence?"

We choose to exist for whatever reason we choose. That's the point.

"I choose a reason to exist? Say I choose to exist to be a brain surgeon, librarian, farmer, a welder, a teacher or whatever. So what? It doesn't mean anything other than I made a choice to do something."

And what choice did you make?

"Huh?"

Which one did you pick?

"I chose to be a farmer."

Why do you choose that?

"What difference does it make?"

Tell me what leads you to choose to be a farmer.

"I choose to be a farmer because I like to be outdoors in nature."

You could do that by taking a walk in the woods.

"Well, okay so I choose to be a farmer because I enjoy being in nature and I like working with the earth and I love creating food and giving people things to eat that are good for them."

And when you do that, does it make you feel good?

"Of course it does. Why else would I do it?"

So could we then say that your intention is to make people feel good by becoming a farmer?

"Affirmative, Sherlock."

When did you decide that?

"Maybe I didn't decide it. My dad was a farmer so maybe it's just what I know."

Lots of farm kids leave the land and work in the city.

"Not me. I hate the city."

So you chose the farm life over a city life.

"So what is your point?"

My point is that you made choices and followed through on them in order to live the life you choose.

"I made choices. How does that have anything to do with every choice I ever made being the right one?"

Are you happy being a farmer?

"Sometimes. And sometimes not. There are days when I don't know how I will have the strength to carry on and nights I worry about where I am going to get seed money for next season, or whether it will rain enough or too much. I get very stressed worrying about that. And I worry that the government might lower its subsidies or that some other country might produce the same crops I do for less money and then I might not be able to sell my crops and I could lose everything."

Is there any part of what you just described that you did not know could happen before you chose to become a farmer?

"I knew nothing about it before I became a farmer. I never expected this many surprises."

Exactly.

"There you go again sounding all high and mighty. I have to tell you that if I had to do it all over again I might have chosen differently."

And you can.

"Can what?"

Choose to do it all over again. Differently or the same.

"Do it all over again? Differently or the same? Oh I get it. You are telling me I get to make choices."

All the time. Every time.

"Yeah but sometimes those choices do not make me happy."

That means you do not always choose to be happy.

"I think maybe it is time to get you a psychiatric examination. I have never chosen to be unhappy."

And yet that has been the natural outcome of some of your choices, as we discussed earlier in this conversation.

"But that was because I didn't know how it was going to turn out."

It was because you did know how it was likely to turn out and you chose to do it anyway.

"So let me get this straight. You are saying that I got what I asked for? That I made choices, even ones I knew would turn out badly, and it's all my fault?"

Exactly. Except instead of referring to it as your fault, I would say it was your choice.

"Why on earth would I make decisions that would make me unhappy? I mean who on earth would do that?"

You might be surprised at the answer to that. Because you are on earth, not in heaven.

"You mean because I am human? And making bad choices is part of the human condition?"

Making choices is part of the human condition. We make them all the time. Even when we don't make decisions, that too is a choice we have made. And our judgment about whether something turned out well or poorly, is another choice we make.

"Are you one of those people who go around saying no matter what happens it's all for the best? You must be some kind of Pollyanna, always looking on the bright side no matter how crappy things are."

I am when I choose to be. And so are you.

"So you are saying no matter how things turn out, I can choose to believe it was a good choice."

Yes.

"Well I don't believe that."

Choosing not to believe is a choice you are free to make.

"Look. A lot of my life has been pure crap. I have had some terrible experiences. I have been beaten. I was in foster homes. I have been broke. My first wife left me. I lost my job. I got so sick I couldn't even work. Are you telling me to look on the bright side, because if you are, this conversation is over."

I am telling you that no matter what choice you made, no matter what the outcome was, it was your choice. And you can wallow in the consequences or you can learn from what you did, and make a different choice or go on living with the choice you already made.

"Yeah but sometimes it seems impossible to make another choice. I mean who would hire me now? I am 57 years old, my belly keeps me from seeing my toes and I never got the right university degree and blah blah blah - you get the idea."

Do you know of anyone who is worse off than you, or who had less training, or who was older or sicker who managed to make successful choices?

"Yeah but they aren't me."

Perhaps not, but we'll come to that later. For now, if you can acknowledge that someone managed to do it, to get beyond seemingly insurmountable odds, then surely you can find a way to find out what they did and make it work for you.

"You make it sound easy."

It all begins with a choice. A choice followed by action leads to results. Even a choice not followed by action leads to results. Although they may not be the results you would like.

"I feel like a total loser sometimes. Nothing turns out the way I want. I just don't have what it takes. God must have made a mistake when making me. I don't think I'll ever get 'life' right."

You are not broken and you do not need fixing.

"What do you mean by that?"

The choices you have made led you to where you are. Those choices were not made by someone with a defective brain. You and your brain knew exactly what you were doing.

"But many of my choices did not turn out the way I hoped they would."

That was not because your brain was defective. That had to do with how you used, or did not use, your brain. Many decisions that we make don't turn out the way we hope because we have not used all of our internal resources in the most efficient manner.

"So how do we do that? How do we use our brains more effectively?"

You begin by remembering that every choice you ever made reflected your positive intention to make you happier and feel more fulfilled.

"But sometimes I made myself unhappy."

Yes. And since you created your reality, you can recreate it anew.

"What?"

Yes. How is it that two people can experience the same event and describe it differently? How can two witnesses to the same event have very different versions of what took place?

"I don't know."

Yes you do. They chose to see what happened based on their individual perspectives and filters. Many of these filters are completely unconscious and result from childhood programming, and some would say, even from past life experiences.

"There you go again."

Yes.

"But how is it that ... well, I mean, how come I don't know about things like this? I know sometimes people see things differently, but what causes that?

You do.

"Come again?"

You do. I do. We all do. We all view life events from a limited personal perspective. Each of us looks at every situation from one 'angle'. And every other person looks at the same situation from a different 'angle'. And seeing all the perspectives from all the angles is really the only way to see the whole picture.

Thus, when 'witnesses' to events describe the same event differently, it is only because they are seeing the event from different angles, and through their own individual filters.

"Tell me about those filters. I don't understand."

I'll give you an example. There were two children who both loved dogs. One day, one of the children was bitten by a dog and decided s/he didn't like them anymore. The other child had always had happy experiences with dogs and loved them dearly.

And then, when the children were playing in the park, they saw a dog jump on a boy and bite at his toes. It was hard to tell if the boy was laughing or crying. One of the children said: "Look at how the boy and the dog are playing." The other child said: "That dog is biting the boy. We should get some help." From each of their past experiences and filters, they were right. Neither of them thought consciously about what led them to have the thought they now have, yet their unconscious minds had created a program based on their previous experience.

"I understand."

"But how can I be sure that the angle I see from is the right one, and that my filters are not distorting the image of what I'm seeing and experiencing?"

It is always the right one for you. Everything that ever happened to us has helped create our filters and limit our perspective. One of our jobs is to recognize this and to be open to the possibility that our view of the world, when we unconsciously react to events, is not the only valid one.

Making Change Easy

You Are Not Broken
You Do Not Need Fixing

1. Is it really possible that I never made a wrong decision?

2. If I never made a wrong decision, then how come I feel bad so much of the time?

3. How can I feel good most of the time?

4. If so many people disagree on how to solve global warming or war or famine, then how can we make things better?

5. How can I learn to witness events from a conscious perspective instead of an unconscious one?

6. Is lying ever okay?

7. If there is only one God, and I do mean if, how come there are so many religions?

8. I am happy sometimes but seldom actually joyful. How can I change that?

9. If the world depends on me for its future, what can I do differently?

10. Does every question have more than one answer?

11. Some people say there is no such thing as failure, only feedback. What would have to happen for me to believe this?

12. Is it possible that everyone is just like me inside?

13. Is there really any hope for this world? For me?

14. What are some of my biases against rich people? Poor people?

15. What are some of my biases against fat people? Thin people?

16. Can I dislike some people and still be a good person?

17. Is there anything I can do right now to be happy?

18. Can I be angry and still be a good person?

19. How can I learn to love myself?

EVENT / DECISION EXERCISE:

Make a list of significant events that have happened in your life and identify a decision or belief that you made as a result of this event. Describe a different decision you can make now. Here are a few examples to get you started.

EVENT	FIRST DECISION / FIRST BELIEF	NOW DECISION
My parents placed me in a foster home when I was three years old. I lived in several foster homes.	My parents did not love or value me. I am not lovable and have no value. Anyone who says they love me will abandon me.	Only I determine my value. I love myself and can share that love rather than seeking to be loved by someone else.
I developed a tumour on my throat.	I am going to lose my voice. I'm going to die. I'll never speak again. I'll have to get one of those voice boxes like Stephen Hawking.	I have an important message to share and I am going to share it.
I was hit from behind three different times while driving.	I can't drive. It's not safe to drive. Other drivers are careless and stupid.	It's time to get on with my life. It's time to end procrastination and to move forward faster.
My uncle molested me when I was twelve.	I am worthless. No one will ever love me. Men use women. I	My anger is making me sick and killing me - it's time to find a way

EVENT	FIRST DECISION / FIRST BELIEF	NOW DECISION
	hate men. My parents will never protect me. I hate my parents. I don't feel safe. My anger is all that will keep me safe. If I stay angry, I'll stay safe.	to heal. I can find a way to forgive and feel compassion for those who hurt others. I am safe in the world. I am loveable.
My sister died when I was nine. She was my best friend.	I am not safe in the world. Everyone dies and leaves you. I am alone. It's best not to make friends because they just leave. If I stay angry, I won't have to worry about keeping people away.	I learned how to love from my sister. She would want me to share my love, not keep it hidden away. I can be more loving now.

REGARDING THE PREVIOUS EXERCISE:

Some people may skip the Event/Decision exercise.

Others may not bother to write down their answers.

You are not those people.

You are you.

Completing this exercise might change your life.

Remember that it is possible to now make alternate decisions or create new beliefs about these events.

Forever.

Completing this exercise is a first step.

Remember:

You have never made a wrong decision

If it didn't work out the way you thought it would,
you were not fully aware of all you were planning

You are creating the life of your dreams

The Past is Not the Future

3.

Making Change Easy

The Past Does Not Equal the Present or the Future

Whatever Was, Was.

Whatever Is, Is.

Whatever Will Be, Well Now, Who Gets to Decide That?

What you are about to read may surprise you. Then again, it may not. This could be because you have heard it before. Or perhaps, you know it's true. Or maybe, you won't believe it. At least not yet.

Whatever happened to you in the past influences who and how you are today.

"But I thought you said we could choose to be who and how we are at any time. So how can you now say that our past influences who we are?"

Because it has. This is not to say it has made you who you are, only that it influences your choices about how you think, act and react. At any point you have the knowledge and the ability to rise above any of your previous 'programming'.

"I know you talked about this before. Can you tell me what you mean by programming?"

Everything that ever happened to you, whatever you heard, saw, felt, imagined or were told has become part of your programming. Every person is the result of a unique set of influences that have helped shape their reality and their personality.

For example, when you watched the television program on the genocides in Rwanda and Darfur, you chose to donate money to help.

"True."

That 'show' aroused a program in you to help others in need. However, it was not the only possible response. Others saw the same show but it did not interact with their programming the way it did with you.

"I don't get it."

Each of us lives a life story. Our stories become who we think or believe we are. The stories we have lived become our memories. When those memories are 'triggered' by an event, we tend to react unconsciously in a familiar way. If the event we are experiencing does not 'touch us' in a certain way, our reaction may not be the same as it is for others.

Perhaps a good example would be a group of immigrants who come from the same place originally and who move to a new country and culture. So now they have a story, a program, if you will, that includes two countries and two cultures. If these people are exposed to a new story/program involving their 'old country', they may well all act in a similar way due to their relatively common programming.

"Huh?"

Imagine a group of Italian immigrants living in Canada who are watching a soccer match between teams from England and Italy. Chances are they will cheer for the Italian team because they share a common program or story about Italy. This is not to say they all would, or that any of them would have to, but it is more likely they would due to their background and experience.

Similarly, even if these people were second or third generation Italians in their new country, they would be more likely to cheer for the team from their 'original story/program' as a group.

"But why does this happen?"

The why is the common program or history that they all share.

The point is that whatever the program or story was in the past, it will impact the present and might influence the future. This is why it is so important to study and understand history. Not to get revenge or gain an advantage, but to become more aware of our programming or our unconscious influences so that we can make conscious choices in the present. This knowledge can assist us to free ourselves from our past programming and to make better decisions.

And knowledge, or knowing if you will, is a key ingredient in living our life consciously rather than on automatic pilot.

"A lot has happened in my life. I have been hurt a great deal and I have come a long way towards healing those experiences and have learned a lot. But I feel there is so much more to life than I am getting out of it."

Perhaps that is because you have continued to live your past as if it is your present. Instead of taking advantage of the opportunity to choose differently presented by your current life events, you resisted the message the universe was trying to give you and simply did not 'get it'.

"My life has been terrible. I feel guilty about so much of what has happened to me and I regret many of my actions and decisions."

Would it be safe to say that you feel both betrayed by life and guilty about how you have betrayed others?

"You read my mind."

It's a trick I'll teach you later. Just kidding.

The other day my wife was talking about how silly it is to regret that past. "It's over" she said; "what's the point?" And she's right. Whatever happened is over and done. The events cannot be changed. We can change how we feel about these events.

Guilt has been described as the 'gift that keeps on giving'. Once a gift of guilt is given, it reproduces over and over again.

"But how do I let go of the past? How do I not get angry about what happened to me and how do I not feel guilty about what I have done?"

It's clear that you have already begun your healing. You went from saying, 'how does one' to 'how do I'. You begin by taking personal responsibility for everything that happens to you and for everything that you do. And once you have taken personal responsibility, you can then make the choice to learn from it. Or if you wish, simply let it go.

"But would it be right to just let it go, to forget about it like it never happened?"

You cannot ever forget anything. That's what your memory is for. You can, however, take charge of how you choose to feel about what you remember.

"But sometimes memories are hell."

Hurting and guilt are feelings, and you get to decide whether you wish to dwell on them. And before you ask it, let me tell you that you can choose your feelings. After you notice a feeling, you can accept it, bury it, allow it to dissipate or dwell on it. The choice is yours.

"I wish it were that easy."

Make your wish your goal; create a plan to achieve it; make it so.

If you did the exercise at the end of the last chapter, you will have already begun the process. If you skipped the exercise, go back and do it now. And write down your answers. It will help you connect with your inner self, your soul and your purpose.

Won't it take a lifetime just to go over all that happened, let alone to heal it?"

As you heal any one past event, it begins the healing of all related events, and not just for you, but for everyone you know, for everyone involved. Really. We live in a universe where all events, past, present and future are related and interconnected in ways we have only just begun to imagine, and are far from understanding consciously at this time. The more aware we become of this, and open to the possibility of rapid exponential change, the quicker we begin to realize our potential.

"Cool. So it won't take forever to heal?"

Change happens in an instant. It's all the stuff leading up to change that used to take time. You don't have to do that any more.

"I'm not sure that I am up to this."

There is nothing you have to do. There is nowhere you have to go. The dialogue has begun. You are a part of it. You cannot help but be changed by it.

"I'm not sure I understand that but I am somehow comforted by it."

Good.

Making Change Easy

The Past Does Not Equal the Future

Questions and Answers

1. If the past does not equal the future, what present and future would I like to choose now?

2. How can I change what has already happened? (Hint: you can't – so what can you do about it?)

3. Have I learned from the past or do I need to repeat it?

4. How many of my pasts equal one future?

5. Will my feeling bad about what happened ever change it?

6. Will feeling bad help me to change the way I feel about a past event?

7. What is the difference between an event and how I feel about it?

8. Is it okay to feel good about myself no matter what I have done or do?

9. If everyone wants a different future, what chance do I have of actually influencing anything?

Making Change Easy

EXERCISE: Who Would I like To Be?

Ask yourself, or even better, with your usual writing hand, write down the question below and respond using the hand you do not normally write with. Write the first ten answers that come to mind. List every idea that comes to mind without exception.

The question is:

When my life is perfect, without any limits of time, money, or health, what or who would I like to be?

1.

2.

3.

4.

5.

6.

7.

8.

9.

10.

Great. Now decide which of these goals or dreams is most important to you. Go through the list one by one, comparing it to each goal on the list until you have identified which one is most in alignment with your soul's longing. Answer with your heart rather than your head.

If it helps, put one hand on your heart while you ask yourself 'which goal is most important to me now?'

And when you have identified the most important goal, proceed to identify the second most important goal. Do this until you have identified your top five goals. List them here.

1.

2.

3.

4.

5.

Well done. If you did it, that is. If you chose to not do this right now, please ask yourself what part of you was holding you back and ask that part of you to co-operate now.

We'll come back to this list later.

EXERCISE: What Would I like To Have?

Ask yourself, or even better, with your usual writing hand, write down the question below and respond using the hand you do not normally write with. Write the first ten answers that come to mind. List every idea that comes to mind without exception.

The question is:

When my life is perfect, without any limits of time, money, or health, what would I like to have?

1.

2.

3.

4.

5.

6.

7.

8.

9.

10.

Great. Now decide which of these goals or dreams is most important to you. Go through the list one by one, comparing it to each goal on the list until you have identified which one is most in alignment with your soul's longing. Answer with your heart rather than your head.

If it helps, put one hand on your heart while you ask yourself 'which goal is most important to me now?'

And when you have identified the most important goal, proceed to identify the second most important goal. Do this until you have identified your top five goals. List them here.

1.

2.

3.

4.

5.

Well done. If you did it, that is. If you chose to not do this right now, please ask yourself what part of you was holding you back and ask that part of you to co-operate now.

We'll come back to this list later.

EXERCISE: What Would I like To Do?

Ask yourself, or even better, with your usual writing hand, write down the question below and respond using the hand you do not normally write with. Write the first ten answers that come to mind. List every idea that comes to mind without exception.

The question is:

When my life is perfect, without any limits of time, money, or health, what would I like to do?

1.

2.

3.

4.

5.

6.

7.

8.

9.

10.

Great. Now decide which of these goals or dreams is most important to you. Go through the list one by one, comparing it to each goal on the list until you have identified which one is most in alignment with your soul's longing. Answer with your heart rather than your head.

If it helps, put one hand on your heart while you ask yourself 'which goal is most important to me now?'

And when you have identified the most important goal, proceed to identify the second most important goal. Do this until you have identified your top five goals. List them here.

1.

2.

3.

4.

5.

Well done. If you did it, that is. If you chose to not do this right now, please ask yourself what part of you was holding you back and ask that part of you to co-operate now.

We'll come back to this list later.

EXERCISE: What Would I like To Know?

Ask yourself, or even better, with your usual writing hand, write down the question below and respond using the hand you do not normally write with. Write the first ten answers that come to mind. List every idea that comes to mind without exception.

The question is:

When my life is perfect, without any limits of time, money, or health, what would I like to know?

1.

2.

3.

4.

5.

6.

7.

8.

9.

10.

Great. Now decide which of these goals or dreams is most important to you. Go through the list one by one, comparing it to each goal on the list until you have identified which one is most in alignment with your soul's longing. Answer with your heart rather than your head.

If it helps, put one hand on your heart while you ask yourself 'which goal is most important to me now?'

And when you have identified the most important goal, proceed to identify the second most important goal. Do this until you have identified your top five goals. List them here.

1.

2.

3.

4.

5.

Well done. If you did it, that is. If you chose to not do this right now, please ask yourself what part of you was holding you back and ask that part of you to co-operate now.

We'll come back to this list later.

EXERCISE: What Would I like To Share?

Ask yourself, or even better, with your usual writing hand, write down the question below and respond using the hand you do not normally write with. Write the first ten answers that come to mind. List every idea that comes to mind without exception.

The question is:

When my life is perfect, without any limits of time, money, or health, what would I like to share?

1.

2.

3.

4.

5.

6.

7.

8.

9.

10.

Great. Now decide which of these goals or dreams is most important to you. Go through the list one by one, comparing it to each goal on the list until you have identified which one is most in alignment with your soul's longing. Answer with your heart rather than your head.

If it helps, put one hand on your heart while you ask yourself 'which goal is most important to me now?'

And when you have identified the most important goal, proceed to identify the second most important goal. Do this until you have identified your top five goals. List them here.

1.

2.

3.

4.

5.

Now the fun part. Explain why each goal is important to you. What will it do for you? Imagine having achieved each goal in great detail. What do you see? What do you hear? Who else is there? How do you feel? What is the scenery like? The more detail you add, the more real it will seem.

Well done. If you did it, that is. If you chose to not do this right now, please ask yourself what part of you was holding you back and ask that part of you to co-operate now.

We'll come back to this list later.

Remember:

Suspend disbelief

All choices begin with positive intention

Every moment is a new beginning

Making Change Easy

This Changes Everything

Making Change Easy

4.

Making Change Easy

Believing What We Value
Valuing What We Believe
And Changing It All

"That Title is Quite a Mouthful."
I Thought You Might Like it.
"I Didn't Say I Liked it."

How we communicate with ourselves is what this chapter is all about. When our conscious goals are consistent with our unconscious values, we tend to become incredibly successful at achieving our goals.

May I tell you a story?

"Sure."

Here's the story. To begin with, I was highly motivated. I became totally infatuated with a beautiful, tall blonde woman who came from a very wealthy background and I believed that the only way I could be with her was to dramatically increase my income so that she could live the life she was used to, with me. Sound silly?

"It makes perfect sense to me."

I thought it might.

It may have been silly but at the time I totally believed that's what I had to do. The problem was my income fell far short of what I needed to reach my goal. So I asked myself 'how could I double my income and live the life of my dreams before the end of the year?' The answer came much sooner than I expected.

Within a week of asking myself this question, I made a decision that I had previously considered unthinkable. I decided to leave my secure government job of twenty years and become self-employed. Who would have guessed that such a simple question could have lead to such dramatic results? That year I earned $279,000 which was four times my previous income.

Yes, I overshot my goal a bit.

And I came to realize that asking myself good questions could lead to having "it all", or what I thought was "it all" at the time. And I realized that when my goals are consistent with my values, anything is possible.

"What exactly do you mean 'when your goals are consistent with your values?"

Let me answer that by first speaking a little bit more about setting goals.

When you have a goal, you know what it is you would like to achieve. And the more specific your goal, the easier it is to manifest it. Of course you have to take action to make it happen. Knowing what the goal is becomes the first step on the path to creating it in your reality.

"Yeah, I have heard all that before. I have taken lots of courses where I set goals and sometimes drew pictures and so on. But I never achieved those goals. They were just dreams that never happened."

Would you like to be more specific about one of the goals you wanted but never achieved?

"Not particularly."

You're kidding right?

"No. I am so frustrated with all this goal setting stuff. It does not work for me. I have heard other people tell how it works for them and yes, I did see the movie, "The Secret", but it never made my goals come true so I think it's all a lot of bunk. People can wish upon a star for whatever they want, but that ain't gonna make it so."

I think I heard you say that you know of some people who managed to achieve their goals. Is that right?

"Yes."

And what is it that makes them different from you?

"They may have set their goals and achieved them, but it hasn't worked for me."

Did you do what they did?

"Huh?"

Did you do what they did? We're not talking about re-inventing the wheel here. If you know some people who were able to achieve their goals, then what do you think would happen if you did what they did?

The only difference would be the goal itself and some of the actions involved. In principle, the process is the same for them as it is for you.

And you might be very pleasantly surprised with the results.

"Well first of all, I don't know what they did. And second of all, I don't believe that following their process would work for me."

Would you be willing to suspend your disbelief long enough to find out if it works for you?

"Okay. Okay. I know you are going to persist until I agree to do it anyway. So let's do it."

Excellent. Let's begin by identifying a goal you wish to achieve.

"At last! I would like twenty three million dollars."

Cool. When would you like to have it?

"Yesterday."

Remember we are seeking to achieve a goal in the future. Our goal here is not to change the past. Not today anyway.

"Okay. I would like to have twenty three million dollars by next Tuesday."

Can you imagine yourself having twenty three million dollars by next Tuesday?

"No."

When could you imagine yourself having twenty three million dollars?

"Right after I win the lottery. There's a draw Wednesday night."

Is your goal to win money in the lottery on Wednesday night?

"Look. This is stupid. I am not going to win twenty three million dollars in the lottery next Wednesday, or ever, so we should just stop all this nonsense right now."

We are only just beginning the process of finding what your goal is and already you want to give up before we even discover what it is you really want. Does that make sense?

"Well right now nothing makes sense any more. I already told you what my goal is and now you say that we're just beginning the process of finding out what I want. Were you not listening to me?"

I was listening to both your conscious and your unconscious mind, and I am not convinced your goal is to have twenty three million dollars by next Wednesday night.

"Well it is."

No it is not.

"Listen. Who is the decider here? I mean who gets to decide what my goal is, me or you?"

You do. And so far you have not clearly identified your goal. Now I would like to find out exactly what it is.

"You're baffling me."

I'll be more clear.

You said your goal is to have twenty three million dollars and you don't have it right now.

"Gee, with those kinds of deductive reasoning skills, you could star on TV."

You want twenty three million dollars but we don't yet know why.

"Why? Everybody wants to have money, that's why."

So you want to have what everybody else wants?

"Stop playing games and get to the point."

It is not really about the twenty three million dollars. Let me suggest to you that what you really want is what you think having it can give you. Is that right?

"Well, yeah. Sort of, I guess."

Be sure to let me know when you know for sure. And what is it you'll to do with the money? What is it that you believe it will give you that you do not have now?

"Okay. Now we are talking. With that money I could retire. I could invest it and live off the interest the rest of my life. I could travel and write and golf and really enjoy my life."

And all that would take twenty three million dollars? Is that right?

"Right on, brother."

And what are you prepared to give for what you receive?

"What are you talking about?"

I am asking what you are prepared to do to get your twenty three million dollars.

"Well I don't know exactly. Whatever it takes I guess. Yes. Whatever it takes."

How much money have you earned so far in this lifetime?

"Who knows?"

You do. So tell me now.

"I don't remember."

Would you believe me if I told you it was over a million dollars?

"No."

It was over a million dollars. You have worked over thirty years and made over a million dollars. Add it up yourself if you don't believe me.

"That's hard to believe. Well, as I think about it, it may be true. But of course I had to spend it to live. I think it would be really nice if we could just get all the money we were going to earn in a lifetime when we first leave school and start working. Then, we could enjoy it all at once. I bet we could live the life we choose if we could do that."

You can. Or nearly so. You can imagine how much money you are going to earn and then plan how you are going to live on that income.

"I think we are kind of tripping the light fantastic here, and we need to take a step back into reality."

If you had set your goal to earn a million dollars, and had an end date for that, and you knew what it was going to take to actually do it, and you planned in detail how you were going to live and enjoy it, and you took the steps necessary to achieve your goal, your life might be very different today.

"I can see your point but it is too late for me to do it now."

So when I asked you before what you were prepared to do to obtain the twenty three million dollars, I take it your answer is 'nothing'. Well nothing other than perhaps to buy a lottery ticket.

"You make me sound like a zero."

That is not my intention.

"Thanks. It's just that I don't believe it's possible."

You've proven that it's possible to earn at least a million dollars because you did it already. And did you know that you can live like a millionaire without actually having the money?

"How so?"

Good question. What is the answer?

"Well, I could live in a country where money goes further than here. I could go to a nice restaurant for lunch instead of dinner when it is more expensive. I could buy quality clothes at upscale second hand stores and rent an elegant cottage instead of buying one."

Now you are thinking outside the box a little. But it is a much bigger box we are dealing with and let's get on with how we create the life we want.

So far we have learned that you want a millionaire lifestyle, as you define it, and you believe that may be possible for you. Is that right?

"Yes."

Good. Now we know what you want. While there are many different ways to get it, would you like to start with visualization?

"Yes. Isn't that what athletes do to help them win?"

It is. Earlier you mentioned you wanted to golf. Did you ever visualize playing better than ever before and then gone out and done it?

"Well not exactly, but I have found that if I watch professional golf on television before I go out and play myself, that I play better." Is that the kind of thing you mean?"

Exactly. Although you are not consciously visualizing when you watch the professional golfers on television, you are taking a visual image of 'perfection' into your unconscious brain and this allows you to perform better when you are playing golf yourself.

I once gave a seminar on visualization and one of the participants had visualized getting a hole in one in golf. And then he went out and got one. I congratulated him on his success and he said was very happy, but after the round he had to buy everyone in the clubhouse a drink. He hadn't visualized that part of his goal and it turned out to be very expensive. Sometimes we only create part of the picture and we get what we want but our outcome may not be entirely as expected.

"If it had been me, I would have visualized finishing the round just before dark so there wouldn't be so many people around."

Visualizing a goal is only the beginning. After we are very clear about our specific goal, it helps to understand what achieving it will do for us. By that I mean we should know why it is important for us to achieve the goal. If it is not really important to us, then we will not likely put forth the energy to create it. That's one of the reasons many people fail to reach their goals - it's really not important enough for them to make the effort to achieve it. And they didn't take the necessary actions to make their goal come true because they were not really 'excited enough' by their goals to actually achieve them.

Having clarified the goal, and then determined if it's really worthy of our time and energy, we can then check to see if the goal is consistent with our values. In order to achieve any goal, it must be a good fit with our values. Any goal that is not consistent with our values will be very challenging to achieve. On the other hand, a goal that is consistent with our values will come to us easily.

"Easily? I don't get what you mean when you say the goal needs to be consistent with my values."

Each of us carries values, both consciously and unconsciously, about everything. For example, you want to be rich. Do you value a rich life? Probably you do. But ask yourself this: "How do you feel about rich people?"

"Sometimes they can be snobs or selfish or even greedy. But they're okay."

Sounds to me like you have issues about the rich that might impede your becoming one of them.

"No, I don't think that's true."

You said that rich people were selfish and greedy. I would be willing to bet that you don't see yourself that way. If that is how you see rich people and you want to be one of them, then you have a conflict between your goal and your values.

"Sometimes you make things seem so very simple. I get that. I want to be rich but I don't want to be like rich people. Sheesh. What do I do?"

It's very simple really. Either you change your goal or you change your perception of the rich. Can you can think of any rich philanthropic visionaries to model yourself after?

"Yeah, but I don't know what my values really are. In fact, after talking with you, I'm not even all that clear about what my goals are either. How can I possibly reconcile the two?"

We talked about how to set goals. When you sit now in the present moment, what does your heart and soul tell you it wants? Say the first thing that comes to mind.

"Peace. Love. Oneness. Friendship. Joy. Family. Freedom. Great health. Money. Time for myself. Helping those less fortunate. Wow. I never thought about this stuff before. Well not like this anyway."

Take a deep breath. We are just beginning.

"You keep saying that."

Every moment is a new beginning.

When your values and goals are consistent, then you can create an action plan that leads you towards them.

If they are not consistent, then you can decide what is most important to you and go from there. There are some specific exercises on the following pages to help you.

"Thank you."

You are very welcome.

Making Change Easy

Believing What We Value
Valuing What We Believe
And Changing It All

Questions and Answers

You set your goals at the end of the last chapter. Now it is time to review your values. A value is what you hold most dear, like health, money, happiness, friends, love, marriage, adventure, peace, safety, quiet, solitude, learning etc. Make a list of values important to you. If you are not certain what your values are, you may wish to review the beliefs you identified in the exercise at the end of Chapter 2. Our beliefs reflect our values.

1.

2.

3.

4.

5.

6.

7.

8.

Well done. If you actually completed the list in writing that is. If you did not complete the list what would have to happen for you to do so now?

Good.

Now, rank each value as number one, two, three etc. Ask yourself if this value is more important than the next value and so on until you have them ranked in order of importance in your life.

1.

2.

3.

4.

5.

6.

7.

8.

9.

10.

Congratulations. We will come back to this list later.

Remember:

Each of us creates our reality. It goes beyond belief

Align your goals with your values

Everything changes when you do

The Big Stuff

5.

Making Change Easy

What About the Big Stuff?

Is Bigger Always Better?
Is It Okay To Be Rich When So Many Are Poor?
Is Happiness Appropriate If Others Are Suffering?

Every thought, word and action results in a response to that thought, word or action.

"Can you help me with an issue that still does not make sense to me even in light of all you have told me?"

Yes.

"Why do people get cancer? Why did so many people get killed by Hitler? Why are people suffering and dying in Iraq, Afghanistan, Darfur, Syria and other parts of the world? Why isn't there enough food and money for everyone? Why don't governments do something about climate change? I mean you have some pretty slick and rational answers for a lot of little stuff, but what about the big questions in life? Why is it that these awful things happen and no one seems to care or is able to stop the carnage? How does all of that fit into your 'it's all your fault philosophy'?"

I was wondering when you were going to ask me that. First of all, it is not *my* 'it's all your fault' philosophy. Life is about taking responsibility. Not only must we take complete responsibility for ourselves and virtually everyone and everything else, we must be willing to accept that everyone and everything may have a path to travel that is not the one we believe they should follow.

"So what does this taking responsibility mean then?"

It means do as you please. Do what pleases you.

"Get over it. This is insane. Do what you please eh. Steal? Rob? Would that be okay with you? Get a life. You are over the edge and beyond it now my friend. You have said some pretty wise things up to now, but this is where you just got off the boat and have signed your commitment papers to the funny farm. How could the world survive if everyone in it was an anarchist and did what they pleased?"

You make the presumption that everyone always does things the easy way. You also presume that humans do not learn from the results of their actions. Throughout human history, people have done some truly wondrous things. They have also committed atrocities beyond imagination and suffered personal harm beyond belief. And yet the community of humans has not only survived but prospered in the long run.

You can ask yourself, 'how is that possible?' and spend a lifetime trying to answer the question. Or you can accept the idea that whatever happened has helped people and societies advance to the point we now find ourselves.

"Here we are on the verge of totally destroying our planet, and perhaps each other, and you can tell me this is where we are supposed to be because, even though bad things happen to good people, that it's all somehow okay in the long run. How can that be?"

People learn from everything they do or think or say. They learn what works. They learn what does not work.

"Yeah but there are some behaviours you don't have to try out to know how it will turn out. Torture for example."

Even torture has its purpose. It has defined who we are in so many ways. It....

"Whaaaaat? Even if that were true, then we, or they, would only have to do it once to get the point. But it keeps happening over and over again."

The thing to remember, whether we are talking about an issue like torture, or being diagnosed with cancer, or allowing atrocities to occur is this: every thought, word and action results in a response to that thought word or action.

"You mean like if I hit you, that you either hit me back or call me a name or turn the other cheek or whatever?"

Exactly. And more than that, if you hit me, then everyone responds to your action.

"What do you mean everyone? "

I mean everyone; everyone on the planet; every person, every animal, every seeming inanimate object. Everyone.

"You have got to be, um, mistaken. And I am saying that as politely as I can. I mean how could that be? How could animals and rocks and trees, heck even people who don't know us have a reaction to something they could not possibly be aware of?"

That is such a good question. Bear with me, because while the answer is simple, the concept may surprise you.

"Okay. But just remember that I don't believe everything you say."

Nor should you.

"Good. Just so we've got that straight."

Everything and everyone in the universe is comprised of energy and are connected. What happens to one happens to all. There are no exceptions.

"Yeah but ..."

Please bear with me while I explain.

Imagine that the universe is one giant being, and everything in it and on it is part of the whole. It's like the entire universe and everything and everyone in it is the equivalent of a human body. And the human body is a very complex organism and every part of it is connected with and communicates with every other part of it. The universe is just like that.

"Even if I believed that, and I don't think I ever will, how could it possibly be true? Who could accept that rocks and trees have feelings or that an Australian Koala Bear reacts to my hitting you on the arm in New York City?"

Not you I guess.

"Correct."

And if you choose not to believe, that's true for you but it does not change what is.

Each of us creates our reality. It goes beyond belief.

"You make it sound like I create my life and everyone else's life too. That's just not possible.

Creation is a process where everything is possible.

"Oh sure you can give me glib lines and quick one liners all day long, but that doesn't change the fact that what you are saying is so far out there that a person would have to travel light years to catch up with your ideas. Hey, I am starting to sound like you."

Why not? We are the same person.

It's only our beliefs and perception of reality that keep us apart.

"Oh really?"

Really.

"So how do you know that?"

The same way you do not.

"Come again?"

The same way you do not. We all know what we know, or think we know, until we know something else. Have you ever considered the possibility that nothing you believe is true?

"Of course not. I can admit that there are some beliefs I have that I am not so sure about but most of what I know, I know. I mean I have no doubt."

All beliefs are a way to explain what we do not know.

Therefore every belief you have cannot be true because you do not know.

"Now that's a logical argument I could take to the casino. Haven't you figured out yet that life is random? It just happens. Not everything is connected. I mean they are not necessarily all connected. Not everything I think, do or say affects you. And you cannot prove otherwise."

What if the world operates according to your beliefs? What if the beliefs you have and the knowing inside you are creating the world that you are experiencing?

Earlier you were asking me how so many terrible things could be happening in the world. What if I am right and you are the cause of all of it? Or at least a part of the cause of all of it. What do you think could happen if everyone on the planet started to consciously believe what I am saying and act accordingly? Do you think the kinds of atrocities and famine and wars and diseases we have all been experiencing could be eradicated? Do you think it might be worthwhile to consider the possibility that I am right and give it a try?

"But it just can't be so. And even if you were right, then how on earth could everyone believe the same thing? That's just not possible. Not everyone could or would ever all believe the same thing."

How many times in life have people said something was impossible and then been proven wrong? For example:

- The sun and planets revolve around the earth
- The earth is flat
- Man cannot fly
- Landing a man on the moon is impossible
- The Berlin wall will never come down
- Polio and many other diseases will never be eradicated

These are just a few examples of how people were certain that some things were true and were then proven wrong. So what harm could it do to consider the possibility that what I am telling you is true? And what good could it do if people began to act on what I am saying?

- How much good could we all possibly create?
- How many wars could we avert or end?
- How much hunger and suffering could we mitigate?

And it is neither necessary, nor even a good idea, for all people to believe the same thing. That would make for a pretty boring universe.

What I am suggesting is that people begin to understand and accept that they are creating reality. What I am asking is that people begin to consider the impact of their thoughts and words and deeds. Are you familiar with the 'hundredth monkey concept'?

"No. Well I think I may have heard of it but could you explain it?"

There was a group of monkeys, living on an island, who never washed their food. They just ate what they could find, when and where they found it, much like all monkeys throughout the world. Then one of the island monkeys began washing its food. This was a totally new behaviour. Then other monkeys on the same island began washing their food too. And guess what happened?

"I can hardly wait."

After about a hundred monkeys were all washing their food on a regular basis, monkeys on other islands began to wash their food too.

"Yeah well maybe they sent a letter or made a phone call to the monkeys on the other islands."

If that's what you choose to believe. Have you ever had an experience where you and someone else came up with the same idea at about the same time?

"Sure. Everyone has, or mostly everyone anyway. Okay. So I did hear about that monkey thing somewhere and it's quite a story, but how does it relate to what we are talking about?"

It is not necessary for all people to think or behave the same way in order for all to change their behaviour, just some of them.

"Oh. How many exactly?"

I don't know. Some say thirty six, a hundred, thousands. Some say more. Some say less.

"What? You don't know? How can that be? I thought you knew everything."

I only know what you know.

"What? But that's not possible. You have been sharing things with me that I absolutely did not know. So how can you say to me that you only know what I know?"

It's true. There may be two of us here, but there is only one of us.

"You know, you are going to win an award for being obscure. Either that or my brain is going to explode from trying to figure out what you are saying. What do you mean there are two of us but only one of us?"

It appears to all we know and understand consciously that there are two people here and that those two people are separate from each other. However, unconsciously we know there is only one of us as I explained earlier. We are all one. We share thoughts, consciously and unconsciously. We can share these because we are one. It is not that our thoughts traverse time and space to reach the other person, but rather they are the identical thoughts shared at exactly the same time by the same beings which appear to be unconnected but in reality are not separate at all.

"Okay. I get what you are saying but there are a lot of people, who, even if they get what I think you are saying, will simply not believe it."

How important is it for everyone to believe everything I say?

"Yeah but you are talking about how we can change the universe and cure cancer and stop war and feed the hungry and save the planet and all that stuff, so I would think it is pretty important that people believe you if things are really going to change."

I cannot make people change their beliefs any more than I can make them do anything against their will.

"But you have to. How else will things change? How long can we go on like this?"

The course of human evolution has never seemed quick by our measure of time, but in the overall evolutionary scheme of things, we are travelling at the speed of light. Or faster. So the time frame for change is dependent on consciousness and not upon the clock.

What we can do is learn and grow and share what we know. Time and time again, history has shown us what happens when one group forces their will or beliefs upon another. So it is a matter of people coming to realize how things work rather than a matter of us telling them what to do.

We can share what we have come to know and understand. And then each of us can evaluate how true that might, or might not be, for us.

And all the while we evolve and grow and learn and share.

"Yeah, but in the meantime people are dying, being tortured, getting paralyzed or suffering terrible diseases, hunger, spiritual and physical pain and so on. And all that, according to you at least, is not even necessary?"

It is necessary only as long as it happens. And then, when it is no longer necessary, it will no longer happen.

"But isn't that like saying everything is okay, even when it is not?"

Everything is okay, even when it is not.

"But that cannot be. I mean why do we have to suffer? Why can't we just 'get it', you know, and move on to bliss or whatever the end will be. Why do we have to go through the trauma along the way?"

We either choose to suffer or decide not to. There is nothing about the human condition that says suffering is normal. There is nothing about the human condition that says bliss is required.

"Well hey, if I am doing the choosing, I am certainly going to go for the bliss option. "

Just like you always have.

"What? Oh I get it. You are being sarcastic. Yeah. But I am a lot wiser now."

Sadness or bliss is a choice. Wisdom is a belief that you are right. And when you make yourself right, chances are you make someone else, or another part of you, wrong. And how right is that? You get to decide.

"I am getting tired. I think all this is too much for me."

It will be until it is not.

"That's easy for you to say."

Yes it is.

"Tell me about choice then."

When you go to the grocery store, what do you buy?

"Well, I buy fruits and vegetables and eggs and bread and milk and meat. What has that go to do with choice? Do you mean I am lucky because I have so many options to choose from? Is that what you are saying?"

Partly. You are very fortunate indeed to live in a part of the world where you can buy fresh strawberries and bananas three hundred and sixty five days a year. There are many parts of the world where the food choices are much more limited. Did you know that in Haiti for example, there is a so-called food product made from sugar, lard and clay and that people are glad to get it?

"You mean like clay from the ground?"

The same clay from which some people might make pottery or bricks is a food in some parts of the world. So you are indeed lucky to live where you do.

When you buy your food in a grocery store, do you ever think about what it would be like to grow it yourself instead?

"You already know the answer to that because you know I do grow some of my own food. What's your point?"

My first point is that one of the choices we have is to grow our own food. We can also buy it or trade for the food that others have grown.

My second point, which is really the first, is that we have a choice whether to eat or not.

"No we don't. We have to eat. If we don't eat we die. So eating is not a choice. You come up with some pretty wacky ideas but this one takes the cake. Or it would take the cake if we were talking about people who actually eat cake."

Have you ever heard of fasting? I am not saying that you or I could go without food forever, although we could probably do it for a lot longer than you think.

"How long then?"

I once fasted quite comfortably for twenty-eight days.

"I have heard about some East Indian Yogis who fast for a long time, but they don't do it forever. I also heard that Mahatma Gandhi used to fast regularly."

Fasting is a very common practice among many religions and forms a regular part of several health regimens.

Within the context of those people we discussed earlier who changed what they know to be true to something else, could you conceive the possibility that eating food, or not eating food, is a choice?

"I'm not ready for that, no."

Are you at least open to the possibility that a person could choose to not eat for an extended period?

"I can agree to that."

And within the context of our entire conversation about things we once believed and now do not, could you imagine a time when people eat only air?

"You're kidding right?"

A tree grows from a tiny seed and becomes a massive object. Where does that huge mass of the tree come from?

"From the ground of course."

No. It comes from the air. The leaves of the tree transform sunshine and air into cells that transform its mass.

"Yeah but it gets nutrients from the ground."

Don't you think that if a tree only transformed the ground into its mass, that there would be a large hole beside every tree?

"I never thought about that. But we are not trees so how do you make the conceptual leap from trees growing large to humans living on air?"

I am simply asking a question. And that question really is: 'Are you open to considering an entirely new reality where what you once believed is no longer true for you?'

"That I can believe. But this air thing is beyond me."

Sometimes it is simply a matter of perspective and context.

"Huh?"

Would you agree that two hairs on a man's head are not enough?

"Yes."

And would you agree that two hairs in a bowl of soup are too many?

"Yes."

So, in separate situations, like humans and trees, the same set of facts can be interpreted differently.

"But that's not a fair analogy."

It's not a question of whether it is a good analogy. It is simply a matter of looking at things differently and beginning to wonder if perhaps our perceptions are limiting our options of how things are or could be.

"Yeah but some things we know are true."

Give me an example.

"Okay. It is colder in the winter because the earth is further from the sun. That is a fact."

It is and it is not.

"What do you mean?"

Let's go back to the sun issue. Depending on your perspective, such as where you live on the planet, sometimes it is warmer in winter than it is in summer.

"Okay I get your point."

That's not all.

"Somehow I don't find that surprising."

The earth is not warmer in summer because it is closer to the sun.

"Sure it is."

The earth tilts toward the sun in summer but the sun is about ninety three million miles away from the earth, so a tilt of a few degrees over millions of miles does not bring the earth significantly closer to the sun – not so much as to affect the temperature anyway.

"Well what makes it warmer or colder according to the season then?"

The sun's rays are more spread out depending on the tilt of the earth. That is what causes the temperature change.

"Cool."

Exactly.

Many things we now consider difficult to understand, or even impossible, may become commonplace in the future. I am not saying that we really understand everything, or that anyone should ever try living on air. These are just examples of expanding on the idea that perspective is everything and that the traditional view of how we eat food may be a choice.

"I can't say I agree with you, but what you are saying is very interesting."

Since we have established that, let's move on to my third point.

"Which is?"

Tell me first why you choose to eat what you do? Why do you eat meat for example, when many people are vegetarians? Why do you choose to eat more fruit than vegetables? Why do you sometimes eat what could only be described as 'junk food' even though you know it is bad for your body and you know better?

"First of all, I eat what I like. I eat what makes me feel good. I eat to stay alive and to be healthy. And I don't think having an occasional potato chip or two is going to make a big difference to my health in the bigger scheme of things."

Remember that we are all connected, you, me, the earth, the air and everything and everyone else. So whatever you eat impacts everything and everyone else.

"There you go with that 'I am you' stuff again. Look, I eat what I eat because I eat what I eat. Okay?"

Finally we agree.

"Huh?"

We agree that you eat what you eat because you eat what you eat. That is my third point.

"It is? I don't get it."

You choose to eat because you choose to eat. You choose what to eat because you choose what to eat.

"But that's not right. I choose to eat because I need food to live and I like the taste."

Ah. So you make the choice to eat because you want to live. And you choose the foods you do because it is your belief that they will make you healthy and let you live longer. And you eat some of the foods you do because they taste good and consequently make you feel happy when you eat them. Have I got that right?

"Yeah I guess so."

You make choices to change your reality and get results. In our example, food is really just the metaphor for the choices you make to change your life.

"Come again? I don't understand."

You are the decider in your life. You choose if you will eat. You choose when to eat. You choose what to eat. You choose how to feel about what you ate.

"Now hold on a minute there. You kinda snuck in the first and last points and need to slow down a bit."

You agreed earlier that there is a possibility that human beings make a conscious choice to eat or not.

"I agreed to a *possibility* that this may be correct. I did not agree that it was in fact, a fact."

Agreed.

"Good."

I also said you choose when to eat.

"Correct. Except that sometimes I get so hungry that it seems I might die if I don't eat something soon."

And as we discussed, many people, including me, have demonstrated that we can put off eating for a long time if we choose to or need to. Agreed?

"Okay."

And we agreed you decide what to eat. And in this part of the world, many people have lots to choose from.

"Where are you going with this?"

Tell me again why you choose the foods you do that you say make you feel good.

"I eat fruit because it pleases me. I like the taste and it gives me a bit of a sugar high and my body feels good after I eat it."

So it would be correct to say that you eat some foods for pleasure and nutrition. And of course, you eat some things because you believe they are good for you. And it is probably correct that you eat some foods because they make you happy: coffee or chocolate for example, because you like the experience even though they have some rather questionable benefits for your bodily needs.

"Right."

So in essence we can say that you eat to feel good. If you don't eat, you don't feel well. If you eat you feel better. If you make certain food choices you feel even better. So we could say you eat to feel good. In fact we make all our choices for this reason - to seek bliss. Would you agree?

"Wouldn't it be counterproductive to make choices that make us feel bad?"

There is no simple answer to that question, but let's accept for the moment that we make choices in order to feel good, or in some cases, to not feel bad.

"Agreed."

Good. Can you imagine another way to feel good? Can you imagine that, rather than feeling good by eating, you could do something else?

"Sure. I could go to a movie or read a book, make love or go to the gym, pray or play golf. There are lots of ways I have to make myself feel good. Of course not everything I do makes me feel good. Some things actually make me feel bad."

What is it about them that make you feel bad?

"I don't know. It's just the way I am. I react badly to some things and I react well to others. That's the way it is."

It is not the way it has to be though. Let's explore first of all what makes you feel bad or good about something. Every thought or action produces within you a reaction or response, an outcome if you will. You then label that outcome as good or bad, pleasant or unpleasant and so on.

"Okay."

Now imagine if you could choose what your result will be rather than having it just happen to you randomly. Imagine that you can consciously select your outcomes even before they are triggered by an event.

"That's just not possible. I am never going to find the taste of squash pleasant or like the smell of perfume or enjoy losing a golf match. It is just not going to happen."

What if I told you it not only can happen, but that it will happen, when and if you choose it to?

"Based on our conversations to date, you are making the point that I am in control, but this is not true. I mean I don't think about how I am going to react to something, it just happens. I react."

It is not nearly as random as you imagine. To begin, let's go back to where many feelings come from.

"Where?"

Many are genetic.

"Genetic?"

They are part of your physical makeup that you inherited from your parents and all your ancestors. For example, your aversion to certain smells might come from a time when that scent or a similar one, meant imminent danger. Your memory of that time was encoded in your DNA, your genes and you are now programmed to avoid that smell. On some level you associate it with a threat even though in this lifetime that smell probably no longer indicates danger is near.

"Well why would I associate it with danger if there is none?"

Do you know how they train elephants not to run away?

"No."

When an elephant is very young it is tied to a stake held by a chain around its leg. Because the animal is young and not that strong, it is not able to break the chain no matter how hard it pulls against it. The baby elephant learns that it cannot break free of its chain. And when it grows up and could easily break the chain that holds it, the elephant does not even try to escape because it remembers that the chain is too strong, even though this is no longer the case. It is not the chain that holds the elephant in place, it is the memory.

"Okay. But I was never chained. So how does that relate to me? "

Your "chain" is your aversion to a smell. It is just a memory that causes what seems like a random reaction when really you are just experiencing a pre-programmed flashback response. And that memory recall in you gets passed to your children through your DNA. It's the same process whether we are talking about smells, food, certain noises or experiences.

"Really?"

Yes. In fact it is passed to your family, not just through your DNA but via other means as well.

"Such as?"

Remember the story of the hundredth monkey? The lesson they learned about washing their food was somehow communicated to other monkeys, even ones that were many miles away on other islands. This reflects how holographic the universe is and how complex human and animal communication systems really are.

"Come again?"

Actually this is a very involved subject that we'll save for another time and probably not even this dialogue at all. We'll get to it, but not here and now.

"Okay"

You have also been programmed in other ways to respond.

"You make me sound like some sort of computer."

That is probably a very good analogy of how humans are taught to function. From the moment we are in the womb our programming begins. We hear sounds while in the womb. We hear music, laughter and arguing. If our mother is upset, we feel that. If the parents argue, we react to that.

"This sounds pretty farfetched. Are you saying that while inside our mother's womb we are affected by what is going on outside the womb?"

Yes.

"Awesome. And unbelievable."

You can believe it. While our parents and siblings are watching TV and listening to the radio, we are being programmed to be receptive to buying certain products and to react in certain ways. We do this because babies learn by imitating and at this stage of life we can only imitate what we hear and feel inside the womb. And of course this 'initial programming' doesn't stop when we come out of the womb. Every word we hear, each feeling in the room is something we absorb and emulate. As we grow into adults, the subtle influences of our surroundings continue to shape how we behave.

"Are you saying we behave the way we do because of our environment? What about genes? Don't they influence how we behave also?"

Both our genes and our environment influence the behaviours we exhibit. There have been many arguments and scholarly treatises seeking to promote the idea that one of these influences us more than the other.

"Yeah I always kind of wondered what the point of that discussion was."

Essentially it's to help us make more conscious and 'better' choices. And all the while we tend to miss the point that it is up to each individual to make their own choices.

"But didn't you say we are all connected and that everything we think, say or do influences others? So how can we make our own choices if we're so influenced by everything and everyone around us?"

That is such a good observation and question! You should go to the head of the class.

"The class?"

It's a metaphor.

You have connected the dots, so to speak, and made a quantum leap to illustrate my point. We are all influenced by each other. We all influence each other. We do this because we are each other.

"I know you said something like that before but I didn't quite get it. Are you really saying that because we influence each other that we are each other? That seems like a bit of a stretch to me."

The fact that we influence each other is one way to begin to notice that we are in fact all one and the same. The influencing goes on both consciously and unconsciously, whether we acknowledge it or not. And as we begin to accept the possibility that this could be true, we begin to consciously create our reality.

"Do you ever stop to think? I don't mean to be disrespectful, but does it ever occur to you that you're just making all this stuff up? It seems to me that some of the things you are saying actually make some sense but a lot of it is so far over the edge of mainstream thought that you really can't prove a bit of what you are saying."

No. Nor do I have the thought that I need to. If it makes sense to you, then great. If it does not make sense to you, then so be it. Either way the dialogue between us has begun. And the more we talk about these things, the greater the possibility we can get beyond the thinking that got us to this point and the more likely it is that we can begin to think outside the box. And change the world.

"I'm for that!"

The more we can think beyond the ways we have been programmed, then the more likely it is that we can find better solutions to things like war, famine, environmental damage and cruelty. The more we open ourselves to other possibilities about how the world works and how we are interconnected, the more likely it is we can consciously understand how it is that everything we think, feel, say and do influences everything everyone else thinks, feels, says and does.

"I think I get that. I might have to hear that a few more times, but I get that."

Good, because that is just the beginning.

"You're kidding me."

Nope.

"I was kind of hoping that we might be nearly finished. Sometimes I think that there is only so much room in my head for new ideas and you have pretty much filled me up to full capacity here. I'm not sure how much more of this I can absorb."

The capacity of all human beings to learn is infinite.

"Are you sure?"

The capacity of all human beings is infinite.

"Well sometimes I feel my capacity is pretty limited. And I am not alone. If what you say is true, then how come not everyone is President?"

How many cooks does it take to bake a cake? How many captains does any one ship really need? How many presidents would you want to rule the country at the same time? Isn't it better when we all work together to achieve a common goal?

"Okay. I get your point."

People create their lives based on their beliefs. They think they are capable of such and such and then make that belief their reality by doing what they imagine they need to do, want to do, or should do.

"Okay. I've got you now. I believe I should be rich. I want to be rich. But I'm not rich. So I am not following my belief that I should be rich. I have not created my 'reality'. Doesn't that disprove your theory?"

It would if you fully understood the true extent of your belief about being rich.

"The true extent of what?"

The true extent of your belief about being rich.

"Are you trying to tell me I don't really want to be rich and that is why I am poor? You'll have to do better than that."

I am not saying that you do not wish to be rich. I am saying that you have created a life where you are not what you consider rich. I think it would be useful here for us to define what it means for you to be rich. And then we can talk about how you have created a reality other than the one you think you believe you deserve.

"The one I know I deserve."

We'll get to that.

"Okay."

Tell me what it means for you to be rich.

"For me it means to live in a big house with a cook and lots of time to relax."

Ask yourself: 'does that sound like a description of a prison?'

"What?"

It sounds like you are describing a prison. A prison is often referred to as 'the big house', cooks prepare meals for the inmates and the prisoners have plenty of time to relax.

"You are being pretty crazy here by comparing my goal to a life in prison."

Wouldn't you agree that many people would describe their life as one where they are living in a prison, one where they have limited choices and not much of a future?

"Well .... okay, I see where you are coming from. But my goal is real and I am not living it. So what's up with that? You said we live the life we believe we are entitled to, and I am not living the life I feel I deserve."

And you are saying that you are not living the life you believe you deserve?

"Are you deaf or something? I must have said that like three times already."

Let me be very blunt here. You *are* living the life you believe you deserve. Everything about your life accurately reflects what your goals and values are and what you believe you deserve. Without exception.

"Well I'm glad we got that straight because I was beginning to think you were making sense for a while there, but now I know better. You don't know a thing about it do you?"

This is not personal, this is reality. And we are talking about the reality you have created for yourself.

"Look. I was born into a very poor family. There were times when dinner was only a bowl of watered down soup from a can, plus a loaf of bread. I remember once there were bugs in my rice and my mother said I could just pick them out and it would taste fine. I couldn't eat it. She said that because it was all the food we had. I never want to go back to a time like that. I want to be rich now. I have done my time in the poor part of town. This is my time to shine. This is my time to be rich. This is my time to have it all. Not tomorrow or the next day, but now."

It sounds like you had it pretty rough as a child.

"It was better than some and worse than others. It was what it was. But it is not where I would like to be now."

Good. That is a beginning. You had an experience in your childhood and you made a decision to create a different life as an adult. Is that about right?

"You could put it that way."

And the life you wish to create is one where you have it all, whatever 'all' means to you.

"I just want to live a simple life in a nice house with a good job and my family around me. I want to live without stress and have time to do the things I want to do, and not have to work all the time spending eight to twelve hours in the field every day. Does that sound like too much to ask?"

Actually it sounds like too little. As the creator of your reality, you might want to consider asking for more.

"I'd settle for that."

Until you don't. But we'll come back to that later. Let's see if you already have the reality you think you want. You have a place to live, right?

"Right."

And you eat three meals a day, right?

"Yes."

And you have a family? And you have free time? And you may not like your job all that much but it pays for your home and food and a few extras, right?

"You are making it sound a lot worse than it is."

Well you are the one who said you are not living the life you want or deserve.

"Yeah that's right. I am just getting by. I love my work but there's just so much stress that goes with it. And my neighbor's dog barks all night and I can't get enough sleep. My kids are driving me bonkers and we can only afford to go camping for a vacation. I really want to take a cruise but we can't afford it."

Thank you for that clarification.

"You're welcome. I have lost track of the point you were making."

I'll get to that now.

Each of us creates the reality we believe we deserve. That reality is not directly dependent on our past, our genes, or our parents. It is indirectly related to them because they contributed to our programming. However, the determining factor at this point in time is the choice we make now. And those choices reflect our true beliefs, values, and feelings about who we are and what we deserve.

"Well I am glad we got that clear and at least we know there are no loopholes here. I mean heaven forbid we should actually act on beliefs that are not true. Look. You have to understand that you have this wrong. It's not that we get what we think we deserve. It's that we get what we get and lots of things get in the way of us getting what we want. You know, things like life, children, mortgages, parents, other people, bosses, credit cards, wars, weather, lack of money ..."

We create the reality we believe we deserve. Without exception.

"Well I guess we'll just have to agree to disagree on that one for now."

We can agree to disagree for now.

"You mean unless we, at some nebulous point in the future down the road, come to agree about this."

No. I mean we create the reality we believe we deserve. Without exception. Each of us does this. When we change our beliefs into knowing, we change our reality.

"Well how do we change our beliefs then? And hey, what about the people who died in the Holocaust or those who have been tortured – how did they create their reality? What about children who are killed? And don't tell me they wanted it to happen or it was all somehow all for the greater good of humankind."

There is no answer to this that you are going to find easy to accept.

"For once we agree."

Our beliefs are at the heart of our experience. Each of us creates our reality. Sometimes this is a reality we believe we deserve, and sometimes not. Sometimes we believe we deserve things out of shame. Sometimes we choose to believe we are meant to be martyrs for others. Sometimes we ignore the obvious potential outcome of our actions or inactions. Sometimes we act with our heads rather than with our hearts. Sometimes we disconnect from our inner knowing and rely on external signs. Sometimes we just plain get it wrong and don't understand why or how it even happened. And sometimes, when we interact with others, life seems to be random, with no apparent explanation. That is not to say that we are not capable of this understanding, just that sometimes we choose to remain ignorant about it.

Each of us is capable of incalculable sacrifice for the benefit of others.

Each of us is also capable of the most heinous atrocities imaginable.

"Well I can tell you for a fact that there are a lot of people who could never do what Hitler and his buddies did."

I can tell you that power corrupts, and that absolute power corrupts absolutely, and that until we come to understand how all people and things are completely connected and one, that these kinds of atrocities will continue to be repeated over and over. Can you deny, that after all the human race has been through, people continue to perpetuate behaviours that so many of us consider abhorrent – unkind words and thoughtless acts, the ethnic 'cleansings', the torture, the wars, the brutality? If we are all one, how can we do this to ourselves?

"Okay. Okay. I get your point. But why is it that humans don't get the point? How many people have to suffer or die until we all get it?"

Consider the following:

- Some people are realizing that what we do to one, we do to all.

- Some are realizing that what one person thinks can create concurrent thinking for all.

- Some are realizing that what one says may create reality for all.

- And some are managing their thoughts and words and deeds such that they are creating oneness in both their conscious and unconscious reality.

"That's pretty heavy stuff."

Yes it is.

"But I think you are overstating the influence one person has over another or over the world. It seems like you are saying that what I think can affect what happens in Mumbai or Shanghai."

That is exactly what I am saying.

"But I just can't believe that."

You can change your belief at any time.

"What if I don't believe this, or that it would not make any difference anyway. I mean so what if I change my belief about all of us being connected or one or whatever it is. I don't see how that is really going to make any 'change on the ground' or at the grass roots level. It isn't going to change the world. It would just be me thinking something."

From little acorns grow the tallest trees.

It is going to change the world. And the sooner you change your thinking, the quicker that can happen.

"Yeah but it's just me. I mean even if I change, what about all the other people? If they don't change too, then what's the point?"

It begins with you. Only with you. Remember the story of the hundredth monkey.

"But I'm like monkey number two. That's a long way from a hundred."

Consider doing the following:

- Examine your beliefs.
- Question your beliefs.
- Challenge your beliefs and everything you imagine to be true.
- Trust your inner knowing.
- Make new decisions about who you are.
- Make new decisions about what is important to you.
- Forget what you believe.
- Act on what you know. Act only on what you know.
- Always keep going. Never give up.

And you will succeed.

May I tell you a story?

"Sure."

More than a dozen years ago, I completed a fire walk – that's where you walk barefoot over very hot coals. The next morning I was telling my eight year old son how it went. He listened attentively and then left the room. About a minute or two later, he came back in the room and said, "I have three important tips for you".

I said "okay, what are they?" I'm not sure what I was thinking they might be, but nothing could have prepared me for what was to come next. He said, and I quote: 'Always believe in yourself'.

Wow, I thought. That's pretty cool. So I asked him for the next tip. 'Trust what is within, not what is without,' he said.

I think I may have gotten chills at this point. Then I asked him for his third tip. 'Never give up, always keep going,' he said.

I probably had a tear in the corner of my eye at that point. I thanked him and wondered how and where he got this stuff. I also wondered who he might be when he grew up. Where did he get these tips? Who knows? Is he some guru guy? On that day, he was coming from a place that we all have within us. It's a place we seldom get to but it is there within all of us. And we can go there whenever we choose.

"How do we do that? How do we go there? I'd really like to be in touch with that inner wisdom stuff. Is there some secret mantra involved or does it take years of practice sitting in a cave in the Himalayas or what?"

Begin by being fully present with what is.

"With what is?"

Be fully present with what 'is' in your life right now at this very moment in time. Pay attention only to what is happening now. Let go of the past and the future and just be here now. Simply breathe and be here now.

And then 'now' is where you are. And within this place of now, you will find the answers and wisdom you seek.

"Is this something I can practice?

If you wish. However, there is no need to practice being or doing what you can do naturally.

"I've heard of gurus who have meditated or practiced 'just being' for years before they became enlightened. So how long will it take me? I am not the most disciplined of people and don't want to wait twenty years."

You already are here and now, right now. All you have to do is get out of your own way and be fully present. Let go of the trappings of reality that you have created. Simply breathe and be. It need not take a lifetime, or twenty years or even more than a moment. And the longer you remain fully present, the more enlightened you become.

Of course, taking action is also part of the process. Let's move on now to speak more about how beliefs create reality and how their relationship to our values can either enhance or hinder the process.

Making Change Easy

What About the Big Stuff?

Questions and Answers

Big results require big goals.

- Take a look at the first five goals you previously listed.
- Compare those goals to your top 5 values.

1. Are your goals consistent with your values?

2. What could you do to make your goals more consistent with your values?

3. Which would you change to make your goals and values match – your goals or your values?

Remember:

Your capacity to learn and change is infinite

Always believe in yourself
Trust what is within not what is without
Never give up, always keep going

Taking action is a big part of the process

Question Everything

6.

Making Change Easy

Question Everything

How Many of Your Beliefs Create Your Reality?

One.

Are You Sure About That?

Yes.

What happens when people do not ask questions?

They get to live other people's answers and other people's lives.

I cannot emphasize enough how important it is to question everything everyone tells you.

"Say what?"

I cannot emphasize enough how important it is to question everything you believe is true.

Earlier, I told you a story about how I quadrupled my income by asking myself a very important question. It changed my life.

Out of that experience, I came to realize that asking good questions could be a key to experiencing conscious creation.

I wondered how many great questions I could ask myself and they just started flowing and coming to me and didn't stop for days. After a while I had one hundred questions, all of which changed the way I looked at life and the world.

And I knew I had to share these questions. So I created a set of a hundred cards, each containing one question.

At a Thanksgiving party, a woman named Samantha chose the same card 'randomly' from the package four times in a row. Samantha put the "100 Question Cards" on a plate and was about to offer one to everyone when one card dropped to the floor. She picked it up, looked at it, put it back on the plate and offered one card (of their choice) to each of the twenty people present. When all of them had chosen their card, Samantha chose one for herself. It was the same card she had picked up from the floor. Samantha bought a set of the Cards and took them home.

That night, Samantha put her cards in a bowl by her bed and before going to sleep, she chose one card. It was the same card as before. Puzzled, she put the card back in the bowl and went to sleep. In the morning, she chose a card at random from the bowl. It was the same card again.

I am no expert on the law of averages, but this is pretty amazing. Samantha called me the next morning and asked me what was going on. I asked her if she had answered her question. She hadn't. I told her that the card was waiting for an answer.

We both got chills.

And so it was with so many people who picked a card. Upon seeing their question, they would say, 'I was just thinking about that' or 'that is exactly the right question for me'.

Employers always ask questions in a job interview – they don't affirm how you feel, they ask you questions because it helps them decide what to do next. And every time you hear a question, your brain automatically tries to figure out how to answer it. For example, even if you hear a person ask someone else what time it is, do you look at your watch? Probably you do. Or these days, you look at your cell phone. Your brain is hard wired to answer questions.

It is part of the human condition to ask and answer questions that drive civilization and evolution forward. You are part of human evolution and will be asking and answering questions for eternity. Well at least until you figure 'it' all out.

Whatever 'it' is, of course.

Making Change Easy

Question Everything

Some Questions

1. Which beliefs create my reality?

2. Does everything I do benefit everyone it affects?

3. What would happen if all my thoughts came true?

4. Am I willing to do whatever it takes to succeed?

5. Am I asking for a lot and settling for a little?

6. Am I asking for a little and settling for even less?

7. What is it I am really passionate about?

8. What would I have to do to double my personal effectiveness?

9. Will I do more to avoid pain than to gain pleasure?

10. How would I like to be different?

11. Can I do more?

12. What is it I am truly grateful for?

13. What is my greatest personal strength?

14. How much of my day is productive time?

15. Would I choose me for a partner?

16. What would I do if I had more time?

17. What is most important to me in life?

18. What makes me feel good?

19. What is really great in my life today?

20. How much money is enough for me?

21. How do I create lasting change?

22. Am I really where I would like to be?

23. Am I asking for a little and settling for even less?

24. What is my plan for achieving my goals?

EXERCISE:

Answer the following question in writing.

What is the best way to change my life?

For example: reading a book, taking a course, seeing a counselor, taking a vacation, doing nothing, getting fit, eating less, eating more, making new friends, asking for help, going back to school full time or part time, spending less time on the internet etc.?

Remember:

Big results come from big goals

Confusion is where wisdom begins

Change is going to come

Making Change Easy

A Sharp Left Turn

7.

Making Change Easy

A Sharp Left Turn

Which Way Should I Go?
What Should I Do Now?
How Can I Really Know?

It is time now to make a quantum shift in your way of thinking; a shift that will allow you to take complete charge of your life by becoming aware of how you interact with every other life force in the universe.

"What is that supposed to mean?"

It means that everything we have spoken about until now, was just the preamble of what we are about to discuss.

"You're kidding me. We're just getting started?"

Yes.

"I have had enough. I want to go back to my reality where everything makes sense: just go to the fields, be with the kids, watch some TV and go to bed."

How will you serve the world?

"The world? What are you talking about? I am struggling each and every day just to get by. Enough!"

Recognize that you *are* the universe.

"Come again?"

You are the universe.

Every thought you have, every breath you breathe, every action you take, every belief and intention you hold, affects everyone and everything. In fact it does more than that. It becomes what is; everything that is, was or will be.

"Get stuffed. If that were so there'd be no wars. No famine. Everyone would love everyone else. I would see to it. See?"

I see. Now it is your turn.

"Right. I want out. Give me my mind back and let me go home."

You are the one making the decisions.

You have, and you have always had, everything you need or ever will need to create your life and the universe in your own image. In fact, this is what you have always done.

"This world is not the image of me. Get over it. I never killed anybody. I never, well, hardly ever, stole anything. I give to charity. And I'm even kind to animals."

The world is not your fault. It's your responsibility.

The more aware you become, the more it becomes your responsibility.

"But I don't accept that responsibility. I don't even believe what you are saying. I mean, even if it were true, what could I do about it?"

Good question.

"Oh you. Listen. I know how the world works. It works like this. You are born, created, create yourself or whatever. Then you live and then you die, or live forever or who knows. I am so confused."

Confusion is where wisdom begins. It leads somewhere other than confusion. Things change.

Often people have gone back to their beliefs, their comfort zone, when they found themselves confused. But sometimes, people will create new beliefs or seek out new explanations to help them cope with things they don't understand. And if they don't come up with a new belief, they cope, like agreeing with the majority, taking drugs, watching TV, overeating, etc.

Remember that beliefs are just explanations people come up with to explain what they do not yet consciously know. And often those beliefs were given to them as children without them even being aware they were being 'instilled'. And most people are fairly comfortable with their beliefs, some of which they confuse with what they know.

There was a time when pretty much everyone believed/knew the world was flat. There was a time when pretty much everyone believed the Berlin Wall was permanent. There was a time when no one believed anyone could walk on the moon. There was a time when pretty much everyone believed no one could fly.

You get the idea.

So what has all this got to do with you creating reality?

Most people who read this will either believe they create their reality or they won't. Some will be aware of "The Secret", or the work of Eckhart Tolle, Oprah, Wayne Dwyer or some Guru type who has explained how it all works. Or sort of how it works because really, you don't know how it's done until you do. Someone can explain it to you or you figure it out or you just come to understand and know. Not believe, but know.

"When that happens I'll let you know."

Please do. Although when that happens you won't need to tell me because I will know as soon as you do. And so will everyone else.

"What? Well I have an idea then. I'll just wait until everyone else knows and then I'll know too. Gotcha there."

Yes you do. You are right. That is one way. Of course I don't need to be very psychic to know that's not how it will happen. It's the normal reaction to the confusion thing. It won't let us wait. It makes us do our own inner and outer work.

"I thought it was too easy."

It is much easier than you imagine. That is why you fail to realize how simple it really is.

"You can spout all the cute little aphorisms you want but that is not going to change the fact that I know more about how things work in this world than you do."

Actually, you know exactly as much as I do. It is when we exercise our mistaken need to feel superior to others that conflict arises. If and when we come to realize that we are all one and the same and that each of us is the other that peace in our time can become reality. In order for this to happen, a major mindset change is required.

"There you go again, spouting off about how everyone has to change, like you have it all figured out and no one else does. Well I have some news for you. You are not half as smart as you want me to think you are."

Actually I have no feeling one way or the other about that.

"Baloney."

Did it make you feel better to say that?

"Yes."

Good. Can we move on now?

"I don't think you realize how radical your kind of thinking is. I mean you want everyone to be the same. You want everyone to love everyone else. You want us all to imagine we are all part of one giant amoeba or something. You want total and complete harmony. I guess I could agree with your goal but really, you sound like a hippie from the sixties who got caught in a time warp. You sound like some ultimate optimist who wants peace and love all the time and that just is not ever going to be the way it is."

Feeling a little pessimistic are we?

"Yes."

Exactly. The only difference between you and me is that you are attached to how things turn out.

"And you are not?"

Correct.

"But we need to be attached to how things turn out."

Why? So you can become a benevolent dictator?

"Well hey. Maybe that's not such a bad idea. Somebody has to make this world a better place."

Throughout history, virtually every person, heroes, inventors, farmers, factory workers, elders and leaders alike, have had the same goal – to make this world a better place. And many of them had pretty different ideas of how to go about doing that. Some of those ideas we would readily agree with while others have left us reeling in horror.

"Well maybe my ideas will be better."

Perhaps.

"Okay. I get what you are saying."

Good. Can we move on now?

"Where can we possibly go from here?"

To non-attachment for starters.

"But we have to be attached to how things turn out. How would it have been if in the Second World War we said we don't care how it turns out? Do you think we would have done what it took to defeat Hitler with that kind of attitude? What about that, eh?"

Hitler was defeated with the same kind of energy he used to overpower so many countries and people. Violence was overcome with violence. And what have we learned from that? We learned that violence is the way to peace. And we know how that one turned out.

"Well what the hell else were we supposed to do? Lie down and let them walk all over us? And besides, after what they did, all rules were off."

There is no question that the nature and scope of injuries suffered by many was great. And had action not been taken, the fate of the world might have been very different. The question to ask is: 'was it necessary to totally destroy the cities and crops and infrastructure of Germany in order to defeat it? And why was a second atomic bomb dropped on Japan after the devastation of the first one?'

Einstein said: 'You cannot solve a problem with the thinking that created it.'

Gandhi said: 'If we could change ourselves, the tendencies in the world would also change. We need not wait to see what others do.'

If you are looking to change your life or to change the world, then the time to do it is now.

Actions of revenge perpetuate the original act. War has continued for centuries because of the energy surrounding it. Only a different kind of energy, an alternate way of thinking and acting can end war forever.

"That's pretty heavy stuff. I mean what you are saying is that it is up to me, up to all of us, to make this world a better place. But how can we end war without more war, or fighting to stop the aggressor?"

Your question is a good place to begin. By answering it you can find examples where alternative solutions will work. You can create new ways of dealing with any situation. It begins with your desire and your intention.

"Well it's easy to know what we want. But if the other side doesn't want the same thing or is unwilling to be agreeable, then what are we supposed to do?"

You begin by recognizing that there is only one of you, that you are not separate and apart. You accept that it is your differences that make you stronger.

"Yeah but what if the other guy just won't agree?

You mean what if they do not accept your point of view?

"Well, not exactly."

That is exactly what you mean. Everyone has positive intent. The positive intent may seem to be money or power, but when you look deeper, you will see where the hurt comes from that has led to what you call aggression. When you recognize and acknowledge that hurt, then you can begin to address the real issues behind the conflict and not just the symptoms. Disease is not cured by healing symptoms – you must get to the root cause before true and long term healing can begin.

"Are you saying that war is a symptom?"

Yes.

"But shouldn't we all want the world to be a better place, a peaceful place, a bountiful place?"

Each person has their own positive intent. We do well now to recognize that and deal with what is in front of us at any given time.

"But how do we create peace if we all have different agendas?"

And the answer to your question is?

"I hate it when you do that. I hate it when you toss back my question for me to answer."

If you want a good answer, then give yourself one. If any answer will do, then accept what you get. If you want to rely on the opinions of others, then be prepared to live with anarchy or totalitarianism.

It is vital that you question everything you have been or are being told.

- Question what you think you know.
- Question what you think you believe.
- Question everything everyone tells you.
- Question everything.

And remember the words of an eight-year-old child:

- Always believe in yourself.

- Trust what is within, not what is without.

- Never give up. Always keep going.

And always remember to:

- Turn every conversation into one that takes all of you to your purpose and destiny.

- Raise up your soul's purpose and put it on a pedestal for all to see.

- Give your full and unconditional commitment to making this a better place for all to live in joy and love in peace.

- Be the creative cause in your life. Be the creative cause of your very existence.

What happened in the past is no longer a recipe for the future. There is hope for the present. There is opportunity for the future.

You are the answer you have been looking for. Look within and find yourself. Look within and find what you have been seeking all these many years. Look within and find your joy. Look within and find meaning, fulfillment and brilliance.

And share all you have learned with everyone you meet.

"Okay. Let's talk about cancer and other terrible diseases then. Why is it people get cancer?"

I am going to give you a completely non-medical answer to that. The traditional medical profession can give you their explanation which I will not comment on, for it is not within my area of expertise. Both explanations can complement each other.

The cause of cancer is a very broad question. If you think of everything that happens in the world as a mirror of society, then the answer is pretty clear. The world often seems to be in chaos and out of control, which is pretty much like cancer cells within the body. On one level it could be said that cancer inside the body is a mirror of society outside the body. It could be said that cancer is chaos within, reflecting chaos without.

And then you would rightly ask:

- Why do some people get cancer and not others?
- How is it that some smokers never get cancer?
- Why do 'bad things', like cancer, happen to good people?

"And what is the answer?"

Cancer begins at the unconscious level of our consciousness. It happens beyond our immediate level of awareness and ability to notice it consciously. This is true for all illness. Cancer, once 'noticed' by the body, is sometimes 'contained' by our immune response and at other times it is not. People rely on their doctors for a cure and healing depends not only upon the doctor's skill but also on the determination, level of consciousness and willingness to explore the nature of the illness and healing systems of the human being.

All disease reflects a "dis / ease" within the body. While there can be multiple causes of illness, our thoughts and beliefs may be a factor.

There are many stories of traditional medicine healing cancer and other diseases. Some people also seek the help of non traditional healers when they become ill. These approaches can be complementary and I suggest going with both rather than just one. It is not my purpose to go into those here other than to say that the thoughts and attitudes of the person can play a significant role in the healing process.

"Can someone ever cure themselves?"

Anyone with cancer or any other 'significant' disease in the body should always consult their doctor. Always. The choice of treatment option must remain with the 'patient', and should include a review of any thoughts that may have allowed, or led to, the 'disease'.

All disease in the body, and every event in a person's life is a message to the conscious mind.

The more effective we become in communicating with ourselves, with our conscious and unconscious minds, the more rapidly we can progress and achieve conscious control of our lives.

"Are you saying that we are responsible for all our illnesses and also for everything that happens to us in life?"

Yes.

"A lot of people are not going to accept that. Many of them are going to be very angry with you for saying it. They will say you have to look at the bigger picture, environmental toxins, stress and so on."

Yes.

There are people who wish to continue blaming society, the government, their neighbours, their parents, their poverty, the environment, the pollutants, pesticides, tobacco, their illness and so on for their life.

Today I read a sign that said: 'Challenges make life difficult. Overcoming challenges makes like meaningful.' Not many people are prepared to accept that kind of responsibility, although this is changing and some people are becoming aware that the paradigm of blame is not working.

People are beginning to realize that only when each and every one of us takes total and complete responsibility for everyone and everything that the world will experience true peace and prosperity.

"I get a little uncomfortable when you talk about taking responsibility for everyone. Isn't that like a dictatorship?"

Dictatorships occur because there is a power imbalance and the void is filled by someone seeking power over others. Dictatorships are not about co-operation and they do not come about through benevolent will. Dictatorships arise out of 'dis/ease' in society and are a cancer, if you will, of civilization.

When we accept that we are all one, then everything we think, feel say and do reflects and represents our soul's desire, and the soul desire of all. And it is through this awareness of all soul desires that we come to understand the true nature of our being and our beingness.

"But so many people have been so eager to follow dictators and leaders and to support some pretty awful acts of violence and greed."

Whenever people have absolved themselves of personal responsibility, and given their personal power to others, there has been tragedy. This is why it is so important to take personal responsibility for everyone and everything. And we must be especially wary of charismatic leaders who make promises but do not deliver.

"Are you thinking of anyone in particular?"

This is not a political conversation. We are not talking about politics.

We are discussing the very foundation of society and our role within it. This role is a sacred trust that must be honoured for the future well being of all.

Making Change Easy

A Sharp Left Turn

Questions and Answers

Now it is your turn to create your own questions.

1.

2.

3.

4.

5.

Remember:

Question everything everyone tells you

All disease in the body,
and every event in a person's life
is a message
to the conscious mind

You are the universe

Once Upon a Time

8.

Making Change Easy

Back to Your Future

There was a time when...

There is a time now...

There will be a time...

Once upon a time...

Many eons ago, in a place where kindness was commonplace, there lived a group of monks. These monks would spend their entire lives from childhood in an isolated monastery on the side of a large mountain, living a simple life working, studying and meditating from dawn to dusk. They lived in search of ultimate meaning.

One day, after many years of study and contemplation, when they were ready, an elderly Abbot would lead a small group of the most accomplished up the mountain into a large cave where they would all sit in a circle.

They sat quietly and the Abbot asked them to tell him the meaning of life.

Each answered to the best of their abilities.

"To experience bliss", one said.

"To help the less fortunate," said another.

"To lead the world to peace and harmony."

"To worship God."

"To serve."

And so it would go until they had exhausted their thoughts.

When they had finished, the Abbot would ask if anyone had anything else to say.

Then he would ask if they would like him to explain the meaning of life. And of course, the young initiates would say yes.

"I will explain the meaning of life", he said. And with rapt attention they awaited his words. Silence enveloped the cave.

He began to speak very slowly. "All your lives you have sought that which you already know, something which is within your knowing. And you have learned much. One day it will be your time to lead a group such as this. In order to do that, you must, yourself, become a master. A master is one who knows little yet trusts that whatever knowledge is needed will come.

All your lives you have sought to know the meaning of life. You have done well. The meaning of life is of course the meaning you give to it. The meaning of life is" ... and he paused until the silence could be heard around the world.

Then he said, "The meaning of life is complete control."

And with that, he put his hands together in front of his heart, and died.

Silence filled the room.

"He was dead?"

Yes.

"But what is that about? What's the point?"

It's about complete control.

It's about ultimate choice.

It's about union and reunion with the divine.

"Really?"

It is not a choice many would make. It demonstrates that we have complete choice in our lives. And by complete choice I mean the choice to live, to die, to create and not to create.

"Yeah but why choose to die? He committed suicide."

It is a choice. It is one far too many make because they do not even begin understand the choice they are making. It is a permanent solution to what is almost always a temporary situation.

Many people are not consciously aware of the choices they are making. Those who smoke, for example, are unconsciously choosing to die over a long period of time by ingesting a known carcinogen.

People who choose not to forgive are filling themselves with 'poisonous' thoughts that may lead to their own suffering and disease.

"But how can this, or death, be a choice? We cannot choose what we think or when we are going to die."

We can and we do.

Many of the choices people make are made by the unconscious mind. Would a conscious mind, for example, decide to ingest a known carcinogen over an extended period of time?

"But people smoke because they are addicted and can't stop."

Some do stop.

Smoking is an act of unconsciousness. In order to smoke a person must operate from their unconscious mind. As they become more conscious, the habit, the addiction, can be viewed as a choice and they become free to choose differently.

"Are all addictions like that?"

Yes. They are running an unconscious program. When they become aware of this, they open up to the possibility of choosing another program.

"But they need help to do that."

Sometimes they do. There is a reason other people are in the world.

"I'm glad I am not alone."

Have you ever asked for a "sign' about what you should do with your life?

"Yes of course."

Some time ago, I asked for a sign. The message I received was very simple but I had no idea at the time what it meant. Of course it soon became clear.

I was 'stuck' at a crossroads in my life and I knew I had to make a change but didn't consciously know what to do or how to go about it. I could not afford to live or support my family and was about to be evicted. So I sat down, closed my eyes, took several deep breaths and asked for a sign.

And very clearly and unmistakably came into my mind the words: 'SUN OF THREE MOONS'. And with it there was a picture of a place I had never seen.

I didn't know the meaning of the words but went to bed excited about the message and wondering what it meant. Later that night I got up to go to the bathroom and as I walked by the patio doors I looked out and in the sky I saw three moons. Three full moons all in a row.

I was so excited I woke up my wife and she saw them too. It was not a dream. There really were three moons in the sky. Weeks later I figured out that the beveled glass in the patio doors had created multiple images of the moon but in that moment I knew something momentous was about to happen.

I was right.

The next day was cloudy. Nothing unusual happened.

The following day was sunny. And that day I came upon the same scene I had seen in my 'vision'. It was this day that I received an offer I could not refuse, and not of the 'Godfather' variety. I accepted and my life has never been the same since. There is of course more to the story. For now, the point I wish to make is that we get what we ask for. When we come from a place of calm, and trust in our inner knowing, a place we might call our soul, we are never refused and always pleased with the result.

Always.

"That's a very nice story and all that but you are still here talking to me and not luxuriating on some yacht or in some mansion somewhere. You are still living what I would call an 'ordinary life'."

The life we live is the one we choose. The one we ourselves create. Are you familiar with the Cat Steven's song about the ferry 'captain' and his son? The father operates a ferry to take people across the river and is content with his life of helping others and 'drinking tea'. The son, on the other hand, is filled with anger and cannot understand his father's way of life.

"Yeah but you don't even own a boat."

A boat is a metaphor my dear friend.

"Hmm."

Are you familiar with the difference between leaders and elders?

Everyone chooses their role in life. Some choose to be followers. Others choose to be leaders. And then there are those who come to be elders. The differences between leaders and elders are many. For example:

- Leaders talk with other leaders. Elders speak with everyone.

- Leaders represent their constituents. Elders represent everyone.

- Leaders take action. Elders observe and follow the path of the unknown river. They know that in the end, the river knows the way.

"So we should do nothing since everything works out in the end anyway?"

I am saying to observe and follow the natural flow according to your soul. According to the elder within you.

"The what within me? I told you I am a follower. I am the guy who likes to watch TV and have fun. I am not the guy who is a leader or an elder. I vote for other people to do those things. And yes, sure sometimes I don't bother to vote but not voting is a form of voting too. I am the guy who follows orders, the one who gets things done, who makes the world work."

Exactly.

"What?"

You are the one who makes the world work.

"What?"

You are the one who makes the world work.

"I find it hard to believe that what I do makes much difference in the scheme of things and certainly not in how the world works."

That's because you are every man. And every woman. You are everyone.

"You're getting weird on me again."

It just seems that way because you are resisting what I am telling you.

"I'm getting very tired."

Sleeping is a way of integrating new information.

"Sleeping is a way of sleeping. Holy ..."

It is what it is. How we interpret it is, of course, up to us.

"Let's move on. So what do you mean by the title of this chapter, going Back to Your Future?"

How we interpret everything is up to us. Including time, space, God. Everything.

"Wow. Now that is getting pretty esoteric. What are you talking about?"

I am about to tell you some things that you will find difficult to believe.

"This entire conversation would pretty much fall into that category."

The difficulty you have experienced has to do with your beliefs about how things are and about how they should be. You have lived your life relying on your beliefs and very rarely have you depended on your soul's knowing. It is your way of thinking and living that has led you to be dissatisfied with your life.

"Okay. So maybe I could be happier. But things aren't all that bad. Besides I'll retire one day and then I'll be happy."

Perhaps.

"Okay. So like what's wrong with working hard all your life and getting to retire and enjoy the rest of your time. Can you tell me what's wrong with that?"

Nothing.

"Finally you agree with me."

I have never disagreed with you.

"So why are we having this conversation?"

So you can find out how to take complete charge of your life.

"Yeah but I am in control of my life. Sort of. Geeze. Now I am beginning to answer my own questions before you do. Yeah, okay, so I am not in charge of my life. It's always someone else making up the rules."

And you gave them permission, so in fact, you are in charge.

"Well things have not exactly turned out the way I thought they would."

What would it take for things to turn out the way you wish?

"Oh my God."

No, that comes later. For now it is important to begin to consider the possibility that you are controlling every experience you have.

"You are very persuasive but let's get real here. That simply is not true."

And if it was true, then what would your life be like?

"I get your point. But are you really saying I am the decider here? Are you telling me that no matter what has happened in my life that I created it and that I can choose a different experience next time, or even now?"

Yes.

"But sometimes someone makes a choice or decision that affects me? How is that my choice?"

You may not be ready for the answer.

"Try me."

You chose to be born. You chose to participate in this reality. You chose to be part of the whole. You chose each action and resultant feeling. You did all this both unconsciously and consciously.

"I'm not ready for this."

Yes you are.

"But you are saying that I have no escape here, that it's all my fault, okay, my responsibility and that whatever happened I created it, and no matter what comes, I will have made it come. That's too much for me."

It will all make sense.

"Yeah, like the day after never maybe."

Or the day you realize the benefits of accepting responsibility.

"There are benefits to this?"

Yes.

"Like what?"

You tell me.

"You mean like world peace, an end to famine, health, wealth and happiness for all?"

Yes.

"But that's just a dream. It will never happen."

How and when it does, is up to you.

"What kind of wishful thinking is this? Do you have any idea what kind of change would be required to bring this about? If all the great world leaders to date have not been able to enlighten everyone and bring about this change, how am I supposed to do it?"

That's a very good question. What would happen if you came up with a good answer?

"I am not naïve enough to believe that what I think or do really makes a difference to the entire world. And there's more to this than some theory about a hundredth monkey."

When you are naïve enough, then we'll see a global shift in perspective.

Did you ever notice that children always find a way to enjoy and make a game of everything? They seldom 'hurt' for long and are quick to recover from just about anything. They are also masters at getting what they want, even with the very rudimentary tools they have for communicating their needs. Do you think they are trying to teach us something? Do you think we are missing the greatest gift that children bring to us?

"You lost me."

Children are our greatest teachers. They are highly focused, generally live totally in the present moment, solve 'major' issues quickly, and get what they want or let it go. Do you think there is a lesson here for all of us?

"Yeah. Let's all behave like kids. Let's just take what we want when we want, play games all day, have no responsibility and eat what we want."

Why not?

"Why not? Are you suggesting kids should be our role models?"

I'll tell you a story.

This is a true story. A couple gave birth to a baby and their four year old daughter kept asking them to let her spend time alone with her new little sister. The parents did not understand this request and worried that sibling rivalry might cause the older child to harm her younger sister. The older child however, kept insisting and finally, the parents relented.

But being parents, they listened behind the closed door. This is what they heard the older child say to her young sister: "Tell me about God. I'm beginning to forget."

"How can you tell me that? I have tears in eyes. That is such a sweet story."

More than you know.

"What does that have to do with children and God?"

We were all children once.

And do you know what else?

We were all with God once.

And do you know what else?

"I'm getting chills here."

Nothing has changed.

Making Change Easy

Back to Your Future

QUESTIONS AND ANSWERS

1. Is there ever any purpose in regretting anything?

2. If I could change anything about my past, would I choose to do it?

3. Does feeling bad ever make me feel good?

4. If I don't create the future, then who does?

5. What is the best use of my time right now, at this very moment?

6. Who are my friends?

7. Do I really have any enemies?

8. What has to happen for world peace to occur?

9. Would it help if I meditated?

10. Is there any chance I could live forever?

11. Would I want to live forever?

EXERCISE:

What steps could I take today to accomplish the five goals I identified earlier?

What steps could I take tomorrow to accomplish the five goals I identified earlier?

What steps could I take the day after tomorrow to accomplish the five goals I identified earlier?

Remember:

Consciously create your life

There are benefits to this

You make the world what it is

Oh my God

9.

Making Change Easy

Oh My God

Could life really be like this?
Like we want it to be?
Like we intend it to be?

You are the Creator.

You are the Creation.

"Wow."

Indeed.

"Earlier, I was convinced you were nuts. Now I am not so sure. Not so sure at all."

Perhaps you like the idea of being God.

"Who wouldn't want to be God? Well, me, that's who. That is one big mega responsibility. That's way over the top. Being God is not my idea of a good time. I mean I could do lots of good things but what about my bad thoughts. What if they created bad things. Killed people even. No, I couldn't accept that. I can see how whatever happens is my responsibility but to see me as God, now that's too much."

How much of what you believe is true?

"Give me a break. I have to be able to believe something. To believe in something is part of the human condition. How else can we even survive?"

Could you survive without beliefs?

"Survive without beliefs? How could that be possible? Oh I know. By knowing it all. By being fully present here and now. But what about the things we don't know? What about those things we haven't yet figured out and continue to need beliefs about. How about those things?"

Such as?

"Well... I don't know. How about... well... I mean how... what if there was... This is confusing. I know. I know. Confusion is where the knowing comes and the fun begins right?"

Now you are beginning to sound like me.

"I guess worse things could happen."

Indeed.

"Let's just say I accept your premise that I create my reality. And I create your reality too. I mean I am responsible for everything and anything that happens, or doesn't happen, or did happen or will happen. That's a heck of a load for one man to carry."

No one is ever alone.

"Yeah but if I am the only one who believes this stuff then they could lock me up. They could put me away for a long time. Okay. Okay. So every great new leap of knowledge had to come from somewhere and was ridiculed when it was first proposed, but really, who am I to lead the way?"

Who indeed.

"Don't give me any more of that me being God stuff. Please."

You only get what you ask for.

"I could totally screw things up. I … I mean I already have screwed things up. Look at my life. What good have I done? How many people have I saved? I haven't even been able to inspire me, let alone anyone else."

You are not alone. We all make reality together. We all make choices together. The more consciously we make those choices the more consciously aware we become. And the more real our participation in the conscious creation of reality becomes. We are all becoming. And the more we become, the more we understand.

"You are starting to lose me there. Becoming what?"

Becoming what?

"God?"

God.

"Well a lot of people would say that's blasphemy. They wouldn't believe it."

You mean they would choose to believe something else.

"Well for them it simply would not be true."

Yes.

"Yeah. But what if it never is? What if you and I are the only ones who accept this stuff? Well smart guy, does that make us the only Gods in the universe?"

Does it?

"No. But how can we all be Gods if we all screw up all the time?"

What is your definition of God?

"My definition of God? The Creator, the big cheese, the One who makes all the decisions, the decider, the dispeller of darkness, the Omniscient One, you know, God, the One who cannot be defined by words or thoughts. "

Can you know God? Can anyone?

"Well. I mean lots of religions tell us who s/he is. "

You mean they tell us their beliefs.

"Yes. Can we leave behind the idea of God as outside of us and begin to know God as inside us, as us actually?"

Yes.

"But who is the decider then?"

The decider of what?

"Of everything, of how things are, of how things will be, of who lives and who dies or what sports team wins. Oh my God. I can't believe I prayed to God for my team to win. I feel so guilty."

How do you know you feel guilty?

"How do I know? I get a feeling in my gut."

How do you know that is not hunger?

"It feels like guilt."

Or what you believe is guilt.

"Oh come on. Of course it is guilt. I have felt it lots of times. It's not like I don't know what I feel."

You mean you have come to know, or to believe, that this feeling is 'guilt'. And could you choose a different feeling instead?

Could you perhaps believe that you made the right choice at the time rather than choosing to feel guilty?

"But I didn't make the right choice."

And if you did, would you continue to feel guilty?

"No, of course not."

Does that not prove that you are not actually feeling guilty but that you are choosing to feel that way?

"But if I actually did something then I will have a feeling about what I did. "

And where does that feeling come from?

"But the feeling just comes."

And then you either hang on to it or let it go.

You choose your experience.

"But how do I do that?"

I have given you some suggestions to help you create this experience. For some people that will be enough. For others, it might help to visit a trusted counsellor or friend.

"Sure. But what are the odds they will think like you do?"

It is not necessary that anyone think or do as I do. In fact I very much encourage independent thought and action. So when you trust your inner knowing to lead you to the perfect teacher, then that teacher will appear.

"But how will I recognize them?

It may not be a person.

Sometimes our best teacher is circumstance. It confronts us unexpectedly: a person or an object we become attached to or distant from. The universe is constantly giving us messages about what to do next. Often we ignore them or miss them. Sometimes we pay attention and we 'get it'. And when we do, we find our lives changing more quickly than we ever imagined and our life changes exponentially.

"You make it sound so simple."

I can only describe what is, as it is.

"But other people have different ideas about this. How can we get along when we all disagree?"

Is agreement necessary to get along? You and I disagree and our friendship endures. And difference can make us stronger and grow tolerant.

Some might say that differences are a vital part of human existence. Although we are all one, we are also all different. It is the sum of the parts that make the whole stronger and more resilient.

Even physical differences that make up the variety in the gene pool enable us to deal with viral or bacterial invaders.

Ideas promote new thought patterns and challenge us to think in new ways that make us stronger and allow us to endure and prosper as a species.

God is all and everything. When I speak of God, I am not referring to any religion, but the omnipresent force that wills us and binds us and leads us to the inevitable conclusion that we exist to create.

And in that creation, in that creative process, we come to know who we are.

And after all, what more is there than that?

Making Change Easy

Oh My God

Questions and Answers

1. Is there more to life than we imagine?

2. Who is God?

3. Why is God?

4. Has God always been?

5. Is there a God?

6. If there is no God, where did we come from?

7. Is it possible that we are God?

8. Is it possible that anyone really knows the answers to these questions?

9. Is it possible to discover answers to these questions?

10. How can we reconcile what we think with what someone else thinks about God without offending anyone, or even everyone?

11. Does that really matter?

12. If I were God, how would I change things?

13. Do we have free choice?

14. Is free choice a good idea?

15. What would happen if we all decided to be God, all at the same time?

16. What would happen if everyone decided there is no God, all at the same time?

17. Think of a better question than any, or all, of the above.

18. What is one action I could take that would change everything?

19. What is one goal that could change my experience of everything?

Remember:

You are your creation

You can recognize the divinity in others

This is where choice begins

Afterword

10.

Making Change Easy

Afterword

Answers to Questions

May I tell you a story?

"Sure."

A man came across a hot dog seller at the foot of a mountain. He asked the woman to make him one with everything. So the vendor gave him a hot dog with the 'works', with everything like mustard and ketchup and relish and pickles and hot sauce and a few other things.

And the man said, "How much do I owe you?"

And the vendor said, "ten dollars."

"That seems like a lot to pay for a hot dog," said the man.

The vendor did not reply.

"Okay." said the man and he gave her a twenty dollar bill.

She smiled and said "thank you."

The man, a little perplexed, said: "I gave you twenty dollars."

"Yes." said the vendor.

"Well, where is my change?"

"Oh change," she said, "change comes from within."

"Wait. That's a cop out. Besides, I don't even like hot dogs that much. Where are the answers to all these questions?"

Consider your limitless ability to explore and create. Replace outmoded thoughts and beliefs with more useful ones as required.

"You really are leaving this up to me, aren't you?"

You are never alone.

We are on this path together.

I wish you joy!

Jim

Making Change Easy

Afterword

What Used to Stop Me?

This will be fun. Really.

When you wake up each day, you can look at things three ways:

1. look forward and imagine a great future.

2. project more of what happened yesterday into today.

3. be fully present.

How would you like today to go? How you experience today is entirely up to you. It's pretty much guaranteed that 'stuff" will happen. It did yesterday. It will today. It will tomorrow. That's not the point.

The point is to let go of the excuses about why things happen.

It doesn't matter.

Let me repeat that. It doesn't matter. If it happened, it's already a past event. Your only choices are to accept it, resist it, or change it. Careful now, because the obvious choice may not be the right one.

If you resist it, then for sure as tomorrow will come, it will keep happening. What you resist persists. No way around it no matter how hard you try.

If you change it without accepting that it happened, and that now it is the way it is, then you will replicate the experience over and over. Ever wonder why wars keep happening? The energy to stop wars is the energy of war. One kind of energy cannot create another kind of energy.

It can, however be transformed. And enduring transformation cannot come without acceptance of what is.

True transformation comes from accepting what is, not from denying, hiding or obscuring it.

So how do we accept what is, especially if it is really terrible and completely unacceptable? In other words, how can we live with the unacceptable?

By being fully present.

Being fully present connects us to transformational powers inconceivable to us when we resist or try to change something just because we don't like it.

And how do we become fully present?

There are any number of books, courses and seminars out there to assist you with becoming fully present. You can search for ideas on the internet or in a library or ask friends and co-workers for suggestions.

Can you do it yourself? Of course you can.

The question is, when will you?

If you are not yet living the life of your dreams, the joyful dreams I mean, what has been holding you back? If you have completed the exercises and questions in this book, you may be well on your way. If you have not, then one strategy may be to go back and do what you didn't do before. And there are some exercises in the following pages that you may find helpful.

Let's begin by looking at what used to stop you. I am talking about the excuses that have gotten you to the point where you now find yourself wanting to change, willing to change, yet not changed. These excuses have probably served you well in the past, and may very well have kept you from harm.

On the other hand, these excuses may have kept you stuck in a rut from which there has been no escape.

Until now.

So go ahead. Turn the page and see what happens.

Afterword

Excuses.

Use them or lose them

What used to stop me?

Excuse 1:

I can't do it

Think of three specific incidents in your life where you used excuse 1 above and write them down. If you like, you can write down more than three and then cross out the ones that don't seem as important.

1.

2.

3.

How did telling yourself you couldn't do it affect your life? Did not doing it make things better, worse, the same?

Ask yourself, in the same situation, 'what if I could have done it?; what if I could do it next time? How would my life have changed or how could it be different?'

I encourage you to actually take the time to write down your answers here, or on another piece of paper or on your computer or tablet or phone. Writing things down helps make them real and connects your body to your mind and even to your soul. Writing things down means you are committed. And that leads to change.

Instead of telling yourself you can't do something, what would happen if you ask yourself, 'how can I do it?'

What used to stop me?

Excuse 2:

I don't have time

Think of three specific incidents in your life where you used excuse 2 above and write them down. If you like, you can write down more than three and then cross out the ones that don't seem as important.

1.

2.

3.

How did telling yourself you didn't have enough time affect your life? Did not doing it make things better, worse, the same?

Ask yourself, in the same situation, 'what if I did have time? How would my life have changed or how could it be different?'

I encourage you to actually take the time to write down your answers here, or on another piece of paper or on your computer or tablet or phone. Writing things down helps make them real and connects your body to your mind and even to your soul. Writing things down means you are committed. And that leads to change.

Instead of telling yourself you don't have time, what would happen if you ask yourself, 'how can I make time, delegate or get help to do it?'

What used to stop me?

Excuse 3:

I don't have the money

Think of three specific incidents in your life where you used excuse 3 above and write them down. If you like, you can write down more than three and then cross out the ones that don't seem as important.

1.

2.

3.

How did telling yourself you didn't have enough money affect your life? Did not doing it make things better, worse, the same?

Ask yourself, in the same situation, 'what if I did have enough money or could have found the resources I needed somehow? How would my life have changed or how could it be different?'

I encourage you to actually take the time to write down your answers here, or on another piece of paper or on your computer or tablet or phone. Writing things down helps make them real and connects your body to your mind and even to your soul. Writing things down means you are committed. And that leads to change.

Instead of telling yourself you don't have money, what would happen if you ask yourself, 'is there any way I can find the money, sell something, take another job, or get some help to do it?'

What used to stop me?

Excuse 4:

I don't have the education

Think of three specific incidents in your life where you used excuse 4 above and write them down. If you like, you can write down more than three and then cross out the ones that don't seem as important.

1.

2.

3.

How did telling yourself you didn't have enough education affect your life? Did not doing it make things better, worse, the same?

Ask yourself, in the same situation, 'what if I did know enough or could have found someone to accept my experience somehow? How would my life have changed or how could it be different?'

I encourage you to actually take the time to write down your answers here, or on another piece of paper or on your computer or tablet or phone. Writing things down helps make them real and connects your body to your mind and even to your soul. Writing things down means you are committed. And that leads to change.

Instead of telling yourself you don't have the right education, what would happen if you ask yourself, 'is there any way I can get the education or experience, or get someone to accept the skills I do have?'

What used to stop me?

Excuse 5:

They wouldn't let me do it

Think of three specific incidents in your life where you used excuse 5 above and write them down. If you like, you can write down more than three and then cross out the ones that don't seem as important.

1.

2.

3.

How did telling yourself they wouldn't let you do it affect your life? Did not doing it make things better, worse, the same?

Ask yourself, in the same situation, 'what if they didn't stop me? How would my life have changed or how could it be different? What if you didn't let them stop you?'

I encourage you to actually take the time to write down your answers here, or on another piece of paper or on your computer or tablet or phone. Writing things down helps make them real and connects your body to your mind and even to your soul. Writing things down means you are committed. And that leads to change.

Instead of telling yourself others won't let you do something, what would happen if you ask yourself, 'how can I do it regardless of what anyone else says?'

What used to stop me?

Excuse 6:

They told me I'd fail

Think of three specific incidents in your life where you used excuse 6 above and write them down. If you like, you can write down more than three and then cross out the ones that don't seem as important.

1.

2.

3.

How did believing others when they said you'd fail affect your life? Did not doing it make things better, worse, the same?

Ask yourself, in the same situation, 'what if I refused to fail or was willing to try even if I failed? How would my life have changed or how could it be different?'

I encourage you to actually take the time to write down your answers here, or on another piece of paper or on your computer or tablet or phone. Writing things down helps make them real and connects your body to your mind and even to your soul. Writing things down means you are committed. And that leads to change.

Instead of telling yourself you might fail, what would happen if you ask yourself, 'how can I succeed?' And what would happen if you believed instead that you only fail if you stop trying?

What used to stop me?

Excuse 7:

I don't know how

Think of three specific incidents in your life where you used excuse 7 above and write them down. If you like, you can write down more than three and then cross out the ones that don't seem as important.

1.

2.

3.

How did telling yourself you didn't know how affect your life? Did not doing it make things better, worse, the same?

Ask yourself, in the same situation, 'what if I could find out how? How would my life have changed or how could it be different?'

I encourage you to actually take the time to write down your answers here, or on another piece of paper or on your computer or tablet or phone. Writing things down helps make them real and connects your body to your mind and even to your soul. Writing things down means you are committed. And that leads to change.

Instead of telling yourself you don't know how, what would happen if you ask yourself, 'how can I succeed? How can I find out how it's done?'

What used to stop me?

Excuse 8:

It's too much work

Think of three specific incidents in your life where you used excuse 8 above and write them down. If you like, you can write down more than three and then cross out the ones that don't seem as important.

1.

2.

3.

How did telling yourself it was too much work affect your life? Did not doing it make things better, worse, the same?

Ask yourself, in the same situation, 'what if I could get it done no matter how much work it is? How would my life have changed or how could it be different?'

I encourage you to actually take the time to write down your answers here, or on another piece of paper or on your computer or tablet or phone. Writing things down helps make them real and connects your body to your mind and even to your soul. Writing things down means you are committed. And that leads to change.

Instead of telling yourself it's too much work, what would happen if you ask yourself, 'how can I get it done?'

What used to stop me?

Excuse 9:

Things will get better on their own

Think of three specific incidents in your life where you used excuse 9 above and write them down. If you like, you can write down more than three and then cross out the ones that don't seem as important.

1.

2.

3.

How did telling yourself things will get better even if you don't do anything affect your life? Did not doing it make things better, worse, the same?

Ask yourself, in the same situation, 'what if I could make a small change? How would my life have changed or how could it be different?'

I encourage you to actually take the time to write down your answers here, or on another piece of paper or on your computer or tablet or phone. Writing things down helps make them real and connects your body to your mind and even to your soul. Writing things down means you are committed. And that leads to change.

Instead of telling yourself things will all work out if you do nothing, what would happen if you ask yourself, 'what can I do to make a difference?'

What used to stop me?

Excuse 10:

I can't make a difference all by myself

Think of three specific incidents in your life where you used excuse 10 above and write them down. If you like, you can write down more than three and then cross out the ones that don't seem as important.

1.

2.

3.

How did telling yourself you can't make a difference all by yourself affect your life? Did not doing it make things better, worse, the same?

Ask yourself, in the same situation, 'what if I could make a difference?' How would my life have changed or how could it be different? How would the lives of others change?'

I encourage you to actually take the time to write down your answers here, or on another piece of paper or on your computer or tablet or phone. Writing things down helps make them real and connects your body to your mind and even to your soul. Writing things down means you are committed. And that leads to change.

Instead of telling yourself you can't do it alone, what would happen if you ask yourself, 'what is it that I can do to make a difference?'

What used to stop me?

Excuse 11:

I don't really care if things change

Think of three specific incidents in your life where you used excuse 11 above and write them down. If you like, you can write down more than three and then cross out the ones that don't seem as important.

1.

2.

3.

How did telling yourself you don't really care affect your life? Did not doing it make things better, worse, the same?

Ask yourself, in the same situation, 'Am I really just making an excuse for doing nothing? Have I given up? Am I afraid? What if I could make a small change? How would my life have changed or how could it be different?'

I encourage you to actually take the time to write down your answers here, or on another piece of paper or on your computer or tablet or phone. Writing things down helps make them real and connects your body to your mind and even to your soul. Writing things down means you are committed. And that leads to change.

Instead of telling yourself you don't care, what would happen if you ask yourself, 'How can I make this important enough to take action?'

What used to stop me?

Excuse 12:

I'm afraid

Think of three specific incidents in your life where you used excuse 12 above and write them down. If you like, you can write down more than three and then cross out the ones that don't seem as important.

1.

2.

3.

How did telling yourself you were afraid affect your life? Did not doing it make things better, worse, the same?

Ask yourself, in the same situation, 'Am I really just making an excuse for doing nothing? Have I given up? What is it I fear? Is it real? What if I could make a change even if I was afraid? How would my life change or how could it be different?'

I encourage you to actually take the time to write down your answers here, or on another piece of paper or on your computer or tablet or phone. Writing things down helps make them real and connects your body to your mind and even to your soul. Writing things down means you are committed. And that leads to change.

Instead of telling yourself you're afraid, what would happen if you ask yourself, 'How can do this even if I am afraid?'

Afterword

What drives you?

~~excuses~~

Motivation

Afterword

Making Change Easy

What's the Plan?

Make a Plan

Don't you just hate making a plan?

Well maybe you don't mind planning a menu for having friends over, but creating a plan for the rest of your life, isn't that a bit much? Those kinds of plans require goals and details and target dates and measurable milestones and ... oh I get tired just thinking about it.

Some may love plan making. For the rest of us I am going to suggest something a bit simpler and less time consuming and perhaps even more fun.

The best plans are the ones that start with the end, where you know the goal. So let's just do a quick exercise right now. If you have been reading along to this point, it's time to put pen or pencil to paper. And just to be flexible, let's do our plan in one of two ways, your choice.

1. Choice one is to draw a picture.

2. Choice two is to make a list.

You can draw a picture of your ideal life. That's it. Sign it and date it for some time in the future when you'd like your goal to be met. And yes, you can use coloured markers and crayons if you wish. Personally I would recommend it. And in case you are thinking that you might feel silly doing this, please be advised that Fortune 500 and other 'leading edge' companies have been known to do this with their employees. It sparks creativity, gets concrete results and it can be fun.

And remember to include yourself in the picture. Include family, friends, wealth, home, spiritual life, sports, health, your work and contribution to society, all that stuff. Have fun.

Draw a Picture of Your Ideal Life

Turn the page sideways if you wish

List 22 Things To Do Before You Die

Didn't I do this before? Yes, sort of. This one is for real.

1.
2.
3.
4.
5.
6.
7.
8.
9.
10.
11.
12.
13.
14.
15.
16.
17.
18.
19.
20.
21.
22.

Afterword

What's the Plan?

Show and Tell Time

What's the point of having a plan if no one knows about it?

I hope you didn't answer that.

Showing our plan to others helps affirm our commitment to it.

You can choose who you show it to of course. You may be amazed at the response. And if necessary, re-read the previous pages on excuses.

Cautionary note: What if the person you show your plan to is not supportive or says you can't do it or dredges up one of those excuses we read about.

That's easy. Just say 'thank you' and be grateful you passed the first test of your commitment.

Move on and have fun.

What Else Can I do?

Be yourself

Accept yourself, no matter what

Re-read the above line as required

Forgive yourself

Trust yourself

Love

And You Could:

Live in Gratitude

Love Unconditionally
(including, or especially, yourself)

Isn't There an Easier Way?

Yes

Accept yourself, no matter what

Isn't There Another Easier Way?

Yes

Here are three simple things you can do that will change your life.

1. For three days, write down how you spend your time. Divide your time into 15 minute increments and write down what you did in each 15 minute period. Writing it down is key. Just thinking about it will not do.

2. For three days, write down everything you eat, no exceptions.

3. For three months, write down every cent you spend, no exceptions.

After you do this, your life will change because you will realize something about yourself you didn't know consciously before. No deep analysis will be required to figure out how you waste time, eat things you shouldn't and spend money in ways you weren't even aware of. What you choose to do about this is, of course up to you.

If you would like to take these insights to the next level, write down every negative thought you have about anything for three days. If you find yourself suffering from writer's cramp, you can do this for a shorter period. What has your conscious mind been telling you? By consciously noticing the junk your mind focuses on, you can begin to realize there is a better way.

Afterword

Making Change Easy

Acknowledgements

Many people, and one pet, have been particularly instrumental in preparing me to write this book. I thank you all.

Marsha Eines, Toby Eines, Richard Bandler, John Lavalle, Michael Talbot's The Holographic Universe, Arnold Mindell's 'Sitting in the Fire", Ken Keyes and Cornucopia, Eckhart Tolle, Norma Toombs, Neale Donald Walsch, Sadhguru Jaggi Vasudev, Nisargadatta Maharaj, Michael Matheson, Ruth Kohn, Toby Eines, Ron Glasberg, Elizabeth Payea Butler @ NLPPossibilities.com, Willow Rose, and Renanah Goldhar-Gemeiner. Plus a dog named Joe, a group of wild dolphins in the Bahamas and every child I ever met.

The story of the 'Abbot' and the 'Four Year Old Sibling' are from personal recollections told to the author.

Afterword

Making Change Easy

About the Author

Jim Matheson loves discussing how the soul's 'longing' and our life work come together to enrich our lives, and the lives of others.

He lives happily in Rosedale in the city of Toronto, Canada. His career has encompassed corporate capital acquisitions, finance, real estate, energy healing, counseling, training and development. After bouncing through foster homes in his early childhood, fifteen career changes in eighteen years, quadrupling his income in less than two months, witnessing the births and passing of dear friends and relationships, literally walking barefoot over hot coals, swimming with wild dolphins and playing with children, he is well qualified to talk about change.

To learn more about his public speaking, consulting and coaching services, please visit www.TheJoyofChange.com or send an e-mail to joyfulchange@gmail.com.

Notes:

Made in the USA
Middletown, DE
26 September 2016